Chicken Soup
for the Kid's Soul 2

What Kids Are Saying About
Chicken Soup for the Kid's Soul 2 . . .

"I loved *Kid's Soul 2*! The stories made me laugh, cry, smile and frown. When I was mad, they helped me cool down. When I was sad, they cheered me up. The stories are all so great!"

Ruby N. Macsai-Goren, 9

"*Kid's Soul 2* is very good because if you are having a problem, sometimes you can find out how to solve your problem from reading one of the stories. This book should be read by every boy and girl."

Mariah Eastman, 11

"I think every kid should read *Chicken Soup for the Kid's Soul 2* because it has the best stories in the world!"

Shaun Michael Arnett, 9

"I loved *Kid's Soul 2* because it makes you understand that there are kids with the same problems as you, and you find out you're just a regular kid after all. This book will keep you turning the pages way past your bedtime!"

Annabella Sherman, 10

"*Chicken Soup for the Kid's Soul 2* was adventurous, enjoyable and inspiring. I learned about respect, courtesy, and reaching out to help others. Thank you for giving us another book!"

Kayli Skinner, 9

"It's interesting and fun to read the *Chicken Soup* stories. I even like to read them out loud to other people."

Antony Olivo, Jr., 10

"Each story touched me. They made me think how it would be if I were the character in the story."

Marissa Peart, 11

"I think these were the best stories I've ever read. I would suggest it to any of my friends."

Donovan Murby, 10

"All the stories made me think of my own life. I almost cried in class (while reading them). I told my family about the funny ones. Everyone, even parents, should read *Chicken Soup for the Kid's Soul 2*."

Breanna Roehl, 11

"I think the authors did an awesome job writing their stories and there were good lessons to learn from all of them."

Whitcliffe Roberts, 10

CHICKEN SOUP
FOR THE
KID'S SOUL 2

Read-Aloud or Read-Alone
Character-Building Stories
for Kids Ages 6–10

Jack Canfield
Mark Victor Hansen
Patty Hansen
Irene Dunlap

Health Communications, Inc.
Deerfield Beach, Florida

www.hcibooks.com
www.chickensoup.com

We would like to acknowledge the many publishers and individuals who granted us permission to reprint the cited material. (Note: The stories that were penned anonymously, that are in the public domain, or that were written by Jack Canfield, Mark Victor Hansen, Patty Hansen or Irene Dunlap are not included in this listing.)

The Summer of Saving Peep. Reprinted by permission of Yvonne Prinz. ©2001 Yvonne Prinz.

Winter Warmth. Reprinted by permission of Alese L. Bagdol and Jeanne M. Bagdol. ©1999 Alese Bagdol.

The Race. Reprinted by permission of Heather E. Klassen. ©2000 Heather Klassen.

Guardian Angel. Reprinted by permission of Katy S. Duffield. ©2003 Katy Duffield.

Kid Samaritans. Reprinted by permission of Karen L. Landrum. ©1999 Karen Landrum.

The Secret Pals. Reprinted by permission of Carla M. Reimche. ©1994 Carla Reimche.

Miss Feather's Lesson. Reprinted by permission of Molly Lou Lemmons. ©2000 Molly Lemmons.

My Brother's Gift. Reprinted by permission of Emily J. Puffpaff and Jamie Puffpaff. ©2001 Emily Puffpaff.

Moms Know Everything. Reprinted by permission of Emily Rider-Longmaid and Elizabeth Rider. ©2003 Emily Rider-Longmaid.

Oops, I Messed Up. Reprinted by permission of Nancy L. Schneider. ©1995 Nance Schneider.

(Continued on page 233)

Library of Congress Cataloging-in-Publication Data

Chicken soup for the kid's soul 2 / [edited by] Jack Canfield ... [et. al.].
     p. cm.
    ISBN-13: 978-0-7573-0405-7
    ISBN-10: 0-7573-0405-2
    1. Children—Conduct of life—Juvenile literature. I. Canfield, Jack, 1944-
BJ1631.C462 1998
158.1'28—dc22

                                                                 2006041165

Publisher: Health Communications, Inc.
          3201 S.W. 15th Street
          Deerfield Beach, FL 33442-8190

R-10-07

*Cover, cartoons and illustrations by Mirtad Gazazian in association with
   Zander/Jacobs Media, Inc.*
Inside book formatting by Dawn Von Strolley Grove

To parents, teachers and others who are living
examples of high integrity and good character,
and who are devoted to passing
on the value of those traits to children.

Contents

6. BEING A GOOD FRIEND

7. LIVE AND LEARN

8. YOU CAN DO IT

CONTENTS

Foreword

Life is so full of choices; you have to decide which friends to pick, how you are going to treat others, whether or not you are going to tell the truth, or how are you going to find the courage to do what is right.

The stories in this book are about real people your age; the decisions they make and the consequences that follow. You will be inspired, energized and entertained. You may even see yourself in some their adventures.

So carry this book with you, and the next time you have a tough choice to make, it may be easier because you will have learned to make the right choices based on good values.

Russ Riggins
President, Positively For Kids! Inc.

Acknowledgments

As with every *Chicken Soup for the Soul* book that we have coauthored, we are once again deeply grateful for the contributions of many who have made the process of creating *Chicken Soup for the Kid's Soul 2* a fulfilling and enjoyable experience.

We could never have done this book as well and as efficiently without the special talents and dedication of our marketing liaison, production coordinator, office manager, executive assistant, miracle worker and all-around right arm, Gina Romanello. Thanks once again for all of your hard work and for keeping us all moving in a constructive flow, Gina. You are always fun to work with, a great friend and a true blessing to us.

To Noelle Champagne, for jumping on board and helping Gina with book production. Your "bubbly" personality, and intellectual wit and charm have been a wonderful addition to our team.

Our heartfelt gratitude to our families, who have been Chicken Soup for our Souls!

To Jack Canfield's family; Inga, Travis, Riley, Christopher, Oran and Kyle, for all your love and support.

To Mark and Patty's daughters; Elisabeth Del Gesso and Melanie Hansen, Patty's mother Shirley, and especially to Seth Reilly Del Gesso, for being willing to give up family time with Patty in order for another book to be created. To Eva, Genaro and Dora for keeping Patty's home running smoothly, and for your love and devotion.

To Kent, Marleigh and Weston Dunlap, for always supporting Irene in her efforts to make the world a better place for kids through her work with *Chicken Soup*. And to Irene's mother, Angela Jack. Your unconditional love and constant support have been huge blessings to Irene, in both her work and her life.

To Dena Jacobson, thanks for keeping Patty's office in order with grace and humor. To Dee Dee Romanello, for your friendship and ongoing support in so many ways.

To Jody Emme, Debbie Lefever, Michelle Adams, Shanna Vieyra, Lisa Williams, Dee Dee Romanello, Patti Clement, Maegan Romanello and Cassidy Guyer, who support Mark and Patty's businesses with skill and love.

To Patty Aubery, president of Chicken Soup for the

Soul Enterprises, Inc., who has always looked out for us with love and support. Russ Kamalski, chief operating officer, for his professionalism and vision—you are awesome and Patty couldn't live without you! And thanks to Barbara Lomonaco, Veronica Romero, Robin Yerian, Teresa Esparza, Jesse Ianniello, Lauren Edelstein and especially D'ette Corona at Chicken Soup for the Soul Enterprises, Inc.

To Laurie Hartman, for being a precious guardian of the *Chicken Soup* brand.

To Brittany Shaw, for posting our requests on *PreteenPlanet.com* at a moment's notice to help us during the early stages of book production; Liz Del Gesso, for your wholehearted efforts and pitching in to help with the Website; Dee Dee Romanello, for your awesome Preteen Planet interviews; and Art Mora, Robert Berardi, Richard Kunz and Al Dewar, for monitoring the Preteen Planet chat room and keeping it safe for the chatters.

To Peter Vegso at Health Communications, Inc., for recognizing the value of our books from the beginning and for getting them into the hands of millions of readers.

To our wonderful, easygoing editor, Allison Janse, at Health Communications, Inc. We are so happy that we got to work with you again! We truly feel that there is not a better editor on the face of the planet. We always feel blessed to have you in our lives.

Also, thanks to the rest of the editing team, Bret Witter, Elisabeth Rinaldi and Kathy Grant, for your devotion to excellence.

To Terry Burke, Tom Sand, Lori Golden, Sean Geary, Kelly Johnson Maragni, Stephanie Jackson, Patricia McConnell, Julie De La Cruz, Ariana Daner, Kim Weiss, Paola Fernandez-Rana, Pat Holdsworth and the rest of the marketing, sales, administration and PR departments at Health Communications, Inc., for doing such an incredible job supporting our books.

To Claude Choquette and Lüc Jutras, who manage year after year to get our books translated into thirty-six languages around the world.

To the art department at Health Communications, Inc., for their talent, creativity and patience in producing book covers and inside designs that capture the essence of *Chicken Soup*: Larissa Hise Henoch, Lawna Patterson Oldfield, Andrea Perrine Brower, Anthony Clausi, Kevin Stawieray and Dawn Von Strolley Grove.

All of the *Chicken Soup for the Soul* coauthors, who make it so much of a joy to be part of this *Chicken Soup* family.

To our friends at Arby's; Ed Gleich and Krista Barton, and at Strottman International; Jill Collins, Holly Peyer, Eric Duncan, Anna Silverstone and Steve Gormally.

Thanks go out to our fantastic team of *Chicken Soup for the Soul* Souper Kids™ illustrators—Zander/Jacobs

Media, Inc., in coordination with Mirtad Gazazian. Especially to Mark Zander—you are the kindest and most talented person we have ever had the pleasure to do business with.

To our incredible panel of kid readers and their teachers, who read hundreds of stories to help us make the final selections—your input was invaluable and very much appreciated: teachers Marcy Miller and Gretchen Dietz, and their fifth-grade students at Seattle Girls' School in Seattle, Washington; teachers Monica Nash and Renee Bain, and their third- and fourth-grade students at Joseph R. Perry Elementary School in Huntington Beach, California; teacher Marlyn Payne and her third-grade students, and Victoria Maher and Jason Titzer and their fourth-grade students at Oakton School, District 65, in Evanston, Illinois; teachers Mary Jo Couture and Jamie Roy, and their third-grade students at Bakersville Elementary School in Manchester, New Hampshire; teachers Mary Frances Tintle, Kate Eagen and Paula Mancuso, and their fourth-grade students of Bakersville Elementary School in Manchester, New Hampshire; teachers Susan Morrill and Karen Berube, and their fifth-grade students at Bakersville Elementary School in Manchester, New Hampshire; a special thanks to Principal Judith Adams of Bakersville Elementary for her help coordinating this program; teachers Barb Frank, Karen Timmons, Suzanne Gramer, and Marti Sauer, and their second-grade students at Riverside

Elementary School in Brainerd, Minnesota; teachers Becky Meyer, Sue Wiechmann, Karen Schirmer, and Brian Stark, and their third-grade students at Riverside Elementary School in Brainerd, Minnesota; teachers Renee Andersen, Helene Danielson, Sue Carlson, Kevin Johnson, and Kristi Holloway, and their fourth-grade students at Riverside Elementary School in Brainerd, Minnesota; and a special thanks to Cathy Engler, principal of Riverside Elementary, for her work coordinating this reading program at her school. We appreciate all of your hard work!

To Al Nomura, for your talent, kindness and patience while shooting the cover samples for the book. Thanks for always being there for us, Al!

To the talented kids and their parents who gave their valuable time and energy in helping to create the cover samples for the book. Paulette and Precious Mundy, Jim and Sydney Anderson, Amy and Noah Bockman, Shanna and Andy Viera, and Greer and Matthew Lobdell, we thank you so much!

To Scott Kline, for dropping everything to fix our computer issues! Thank you.

Most of all, our gratitude goes out to everyone who submitted heartfelt stories, poems, quotes and cartoons for possible inclusion in this book. We especially thank the Society of Children's Book Writers and Illustrators for always sending such well-written and age-appropriate material for us to consider.

Finally, thanks to all the kids and preteens who take

time to write to us just to say how much they love *Chicken Soup for the Kid's Soul, Preteen Soul, Preteen Soul 2 and Girl's Soul.* Your letters fuel our passion to help you through your preteen years by sharing true life stories with you. Again, it means the world to us to hear how our books have changed your lives for the better.

Because of the size of this project, we may have left out the names of some people who contributed along the way. If so, we are sorry, but please know that we really do appreciate you very much.

We are truly grateful, and we love you all!

Introduction

In today's world of busy parents and teachers, and in many cases, busier kids, it's sometimes hard to stop long enough in our daily routines to find those valuable windows of time needed to share ageless bits of wisdom. Sometimes, it's even harder to find the wisdom to share. And with myriad mixed-up messages being thrown at kids today about what matters in life, teaching good character seems to be a constant battle.

In our material world, the message that "looking out for number one" as the key to happiness seems to prevail. But encouraging kids to make healthy choices that are beneficial, not only to them but to others as well, is a far more powerful message—and these are the choices that lead to satisfaction, happiness, fulfillment and success in life.

And that's just what *Chicken Soup for the Kid's Soul 2* has to offer. *Kid's Soul 2*, a book for six- to ten-year-olds, is built upon the true experiences of others who have learned positive character trait lessons by having lived them. Each message is wrapped up in a short story that might have taken years to learn, but will take only minutes for a parent or teacher to read to a child, or for an older child to read alone. These stories teach without preaching about the importance of being honest, kind and understanding.

When these stories are shared, whether in the home or in the classroom, they create a neutral, non-threatening platform that can launch discussions about issues that kids face. Sharing *Kid's Soul 2* stories can also segue into the sharing of your own personal history or family stories that have been handed down from generation to generation.

To make this book even more engaging and kid-friendly, we are presenting customized *Chicken Soup for the Soul* Souper Kids™ cartoons and illustrations specifically designed to support the stories and themes. Please encourage your kids to check out the Souper Kids Cartoon Collection at the back of the book.

These stories, along with the Souper Kids, will empower kids to persevere, be a better friend, find their courage, initiate kind deeds, and become the kind of person whom others embrace and respect. And for a parent or teacher to be able to impart that to a child is an immeasurably wonderful gift.

So, take a few minutes and share a character-building

life experience from *Chicken Soup for the Kid's Soul 2*
with a child in your life. We're sure you'll be glad that
you did.

Share with Us

We would like to know how these stories affected you and which ones were your favorites. Please write to us and let us know.

Also, please send us your nonfiction stories and poems that you would like us to consider for future books.

E-mail us at *mail@lifewriters.com*

Chicken Soup for the Kid's Soul 2
Attn: Patty Hansen and Irene Dunlap
P.O. Box 10879
Costa Mesa, CA 92627
Visit our Websites at:
www.lifewriters.com
www.preteenplanet.com
www.chickensoup.com

1

BEING KIND

Love and kindness are never wasted.
They always make a difference.
They bless the one who receives them,
And they bless you,
The giver.

Barbara De Angelis

The Summer of Saving Peep

Three things in human life are important. The first is to be kind. The second is to be kind. And the third is to be kind.

Henry James

One sunny afternoon in June, my sister Jenny and I were walking home from school when we noticed a loud chirping coming from an empty trashcan on the curb. We walked over to it and peered inside. A sad little sparrow was sitting at the bottom of the trashcan, chirping his heart out. His right wing stuck out from his body at a strange angle. Jenny said it was probably broken. She reached in and cupped the bird in her hands, cooing to him so he wouldn't be scared. The sparrow chirped all the way to our house, his little, fuzzy head poking through Jenny's fingers.

My mom took one look at the little bird and said, "No way! I'm not having another animal in the house." But once she got a closer look at those big, sad eyes and heard that pathetic chirping, her heart melted. We were counting on that.

Mom sent me into the bathroom for tape and an eyedropper and gently set the sparrow on the kitchen table to get a better look at him. She said his right wing was definitely broken, so she designed a splint out of a Popsicle stick and carefully taped it to his wing. Our dog, Buttons, kept trying to get a look at the bird, but we shooed her away.

Once the splint was on, we fed the bird water with an eyedropper and gave him bits of bread and berries. At first he wouldn't eat, but then after awhile, he wouldn't stop.

The little bird earned the name Peep. We kept him in an old hamster cage, former home of Pepper, the hamster, who'd recently passed away from old age. Every night, we put a towel over the cage, and Peep went right to sleep. And every morning, we put his cage outside and opened the door so he could wander around and get some fresh air. Peep couldn't fly, which seemed to frustrate him. He wasn't used to walking everywhere. Eventually, Peep made friends with Buttons. I swear it's true! Peep would jump onto Buttons' back for a free ride around the back yard.

After awhile, Peep's wing got better, and Mom told us it was probably time to take off the splint. We put Peep on the kitchen table, and Mom cut off most of the splint with little scissors. She couldn't get all of it, so there were bits of white tape stuck to his wing, but he didn't seem to mind. He started flapping his wing like crazy, and the next morning when we opened the cage door, he flew about fifty feet into the air before coming back. We watched from the ground like proud parents. From then on, Peep flew further each morning, but he always came back.

Two weeks later, on a Sunday morning, when Jenny let Peep out of his cage, he just kept flying. We left his cage outside with the door open, but he never came home all that day. As it became dark, we faced the truth that Peep would never come back. My mom said he probably found some other sparrows and decided it was time to be with his own kind. My eyes filled with tears, and so did Jenny's. We all missed Peep a lot—even Buttons, who paced around in front of his cage every morning for weeks.

A few months later, Jenny and I were walking home from school, and a sparrow landed on a low tree branch just ahead of where we were walking. We both stopped and stared at it, amazed. The bird had little bits of white tape stuck to his right wing.

Jenny and I didn't say a word to each other. Peep sat on the branch chirping at us for a couple of seconds, and then he flew off. We watched him join a little flock of sparrows and disappear into the sky with them. We decided that it wasn't one of those crazy coincidences. Peep had come to say a proper good-bye and to thank us for saving his life.

Yvonne Prinz

Winter Warmth

When you carry out acts of kindness, you get a wonderful feeling inside. It is as though something inside your body responds and says, yes, this is how I ought to feel.

Harold Kushner

Whoosh! Ahhhh . . . the sound of my sled sliding on top of the snow! It was what I had been looking forward to ever since the beginning of winter.

It was a long hike up to the top of the snow hill, the snow crunching under my boots. My arms ached from pulling the sled. The wind tore at my face, and my eyes filled with tears from the cold wind. But it would all be worth it in a minute.

I got to the top of the hill and lay stomach-down on the sled to begin the fast trip down. Everything was a blur as I flew down the hill. Whoosh! There's that great sound! Then I saw something out of the corner of my eye.

When I got to the bottom of the hill, I looked around for what had caught my attention. Then, I saw a woman pushing a shopping cart. The snow-covered sidewalk made it hard for her to walk. As she got closer, I noticed that she had on several thin coats and a couple of hats, and her fingers were showing through her gloves. I knew in an instant that she was a homeless person. She looked very tired, cold and helpless. My heart sank. How could I be enjoying this weather that someone else was dreading?

I watched her struggle to push the cart. I wanted to help her, but what could I do? Then I remembered the church at the top of the hill.

I ran up the hill, dragging the sled through the parking lot and into the church. I saw a man cleaning the floor, and I told him about the woman. He followed me outside. The woman was still struggling up the sidewalk with the cart. The man walked up to her and told her not to be afraid, that he worked at the church and he could help her. He said that the church was taking in homeless people for the weekend, and she was welcome to come inside, have something to eat and get warm.

The homeless woman looked so grateful! I felt so good that I couldn't stop smiling.

When I went outside, snow was falling softly, and it made me feel peaceful. Once again, I lay on my stomach and started down the hill. Only this time, the wind seemed gentle, my eyes didn't water from the cold, and I felt warm inside. What a great day!

Alese Bagdol, 11

The Race

It is our choices . . . that show what we truly are, far more than our abilities.

J. K. Rowling

Todd and Brett maneuvered their milk-carton boat to the starting line.

"This is it, Todd," Brett said, dipping his oar into the water. "This year we have to win. We've built the best boat out here."

Todd nodded. "We'd better win," he said. "Since we're twelve now, it's our last year to be in the kids' division. Next year the competition will be a lot tougher."

"Yeah," Brett agreed. "No second place for us this year. Right, Todd?"

Todd nodded again and slapped the side of the boat. He and Brett had worked for months in Brett's garage, waterproofing each milk carton before assembling the hundreds of cartons into this streamlined racing boat—as streamlined as boxy milk cartons would allow. The boat construction had to follow all the rules that the Dairy Association, the group that sponsored the race on the lake, made for the annual event.

"The competition this year doesn't look tough at all," Brett said. "But when the race starts, Todd, we need to pour it on and not let up until we cross that finish line."

"Sure," Todd agreed, glancing up and down the line of boats positioned at the starting line. Part of the fun of the race was just to see all the crazy boats other kids had constructed out of milk cartons. Todd looked at the boat next to his and Brett's. The owner was a little kid, probably not more than eight—the minimum age for the race—and he was struggling to keep his boat from drifting away from the starting line.

"Look, Brett," Todd said, poking Brett with the end of his oar. "That little kid is here all by himself."

"Looks like he built the boat all by himself, too," Brett replied. "How does he expect to get anywhere in that wreck?"

That boat does look pretty bad, Todd thought. He shook his head, thinking of all the hours and effort the boy must have put into making his boat.

Suddenly, the whistle blew. The race had begun. Todd dipped his oar into the water and stroked, watching Brett, sitting in front of him, do the same. Their boat glided quickly out in front of the others.

"Keep going. We're ahead!" Brett shouted, as he and

Todd paddled through the water.

We're winning! Todd thought, as he glanced quickly to both sides. *No one else is even near us.* In the distance, Todd could see the finish line. They had quite a way to go in the long race, but at least they were ahead. Todd took a quick break from stroking and looked back over his shoulder, curious to see how the little boy who had been next to them was doing.

"Brett," Todd yelled, "that little kid has barely moved from the starting line. And he's drifting off to the side. He can hardly control his boat."

"So what?" Brett threw the words over his shoulder. "We're winning!"

Yeah, we're winning, Todd silently agreed with Brett, but all he could think of was the year when he and Brett were nine, and they had entered the milk-carton race for the first time. They didn't have any idea about what they were doing, their boat was a disaster, and they never even reached the finish line before sinking. Todd remembered how he and Brett had fought back tears as they watched their dreams sink beneath the water.

"We have to help him!" Todd yelled.

"Are you crazy?!?" Brett took a break from rowing to turn around and scowl at Todd. "We have this race won. That is, if you keep rowing. We're not stopping for anything, Todd. Especially not some little kid who doesn't even know how to do anything right."

"I just remember when we were like that little kid," Todd said. "And I'm going to help him—even if you're not." Todd set down his oar and swung his legs over the side of the boat, ready to jump into the water.

"Wait!" Brett yelled. "If you leave me alone on this boat, we can't win the race!"

"But if you help me with that kid's boat, we can all cross the finish line," Todd said evenly.

Brett stared at his friend, then watched as another boat began to gain on them. "This is lame," Brett replied, "but I guess I have no choice. Let's turn around and get him."

Together, Todd and Brett turned the boat around and quickly cut through the water to reach the little boy. The boy had barely made it past the starting line, his boat drifting toward the center of the lake, with no hope of ever reaching the finish line.

"Throw us your tow rope," Todd called as they reached the boy's boat. The boy looked at Todd through eyes that were close to tears and tossed him the rope. Todd grabbed the rope and wrapped it through the tow hook on their boat.

"Okay, go!" Todd called to Brett.

As Todd dipped his oar into the water, he called back to the boy, "We'll get you to that finish line."

"I still think this is lame," Brett said. "We would've won, Todd. Now we've lost for sure." Brett pointed out the dozen or so boats ahead of them in the water, certain to cross the finish line before they did. Todd glanced back at the little boy, who now stroked the water with his oar, finally heading in the right direction.

"Thanks," the boy said to Todd. "I never would have

made it without your help. But I'm sorry you're not going to win now."

"That's okay," Todd said. "Winning isn't everything."

And as the little boy looked at Todd and smiled, Todd knew that he meant it.

Heather Klassen

Guardian Angel

Forget injuries; never forget kindness.

Confucius

"That new girl is staring at us again," my best friend Sherri said.

Looking across the crowded cafeteria full of sixth-graders, I saw the girl hunched over the table, sitting all alone. When she looked in our direction, I waved.

"What are you doing?" Sherri cried, grabbing my arm.

"How would you feel if you were the new kid?" I asked. "Besides, I've been watching her all week. She never eats anything."

I motioned to the girl again.

Slowly she slipped from her seat. Her wrinkled jeans looked about two sizes too big. Brown, stringy hair covered most of her face. When she reached our table, she stood there staring down at her worn-out flip-flops.

"Hi," I said. "I'm Katy, and this is Sherri."

"Hi," she said softly. "My name's Carlotta."

"Want to eat with us?" I asked.

Carlotta's head jerked up. A small smile crept across her lips.

"My mom packed two sandwiches today. She has this crazy idea that I need to gain weight," I explained. "But I'll never eat two. Do you want one?"

"Are you sure?" she asked.

I slid the second sandwich over to her.

That afternoon I invited Carlotta to come home with me. In my room, she looked at my photographs, and then began admiring my earring collection. When she picked up my favorite pair of gold angel earrings, she said, "I've never seen anything so beautiful."

"Thanks," I told her. "Those are my guardian angels."

After a trip to the kitchen, I came back to my room and offered her a snack.

"No, thanks," she mumbled. "I need to go."

Carlotta pushed past me toward the door.

"Hey, wait!" I said, hurrying after her.

"See you tomorrow," she called as she rushed down the front walk.

"I won't be at school tomorrow," I yelled after her. "But I'll see you Thursday. And, if you want, I'll bring an extra sandwich."

"Thanks, Katy," she said. "My mom lost her job a few weeks ago, and money is kind of tight." She turned and ran down the sidewalk.

The next morning at school, I saw Carlotta in the hallway. "Wait up!" I yelled.

Carlotta whirled around. "I . . . uh . . . I thought you weren't going to be here today," she stuttered.

"I was supposed to go to the dentist, but Mom had to cancel my appointment."

"I better go," Carlotta said, turning her back on me.

"Wait," I said again. I grabbed her arm and spun her around. My mouth fell open. Gold angel earrings hung from her ears. She jerked her arm away from me and raced down the hall.

Anger boiled over deep inside me. *How could she? I'd just tried to be her friend and this is the thanks I get?*

Later that afternoon, I got a phone call. When I put the phone to my ear, I heard sniffles.

"Katy?" Carlotta whispered.

"What do you want?" I said angrily.

"I'm sorry about the earrings," she replied, her voice cracking.

"Sure you are," I said. "I was only trying to be your friend."

"I know."

After a long silence, Carlotta said, "I have to go. I'm on a pay phone. I don't have a way to bring your earrings back, but if your mom can bring you by, I live at Meadowlake Trailer Park, Number 54."

I slammed down the phone. But later, as I thought about Carlotta in her hand-me-down clothes, carrying an empty lunch sack, I felt the anger sliding away. I knew I had a choice to make. I could either waste my energy being mad, or I could try to help.

After gathering some things, I filled my mom in on what had happened and asked if she would take me to Carlotta's.

A few minutes later, we pulled down the dusty dirt road into the trailer park. When we reached number 54, I took a deep breath. It was an old, singlewide trailer with peeling paint and cardboard covering a broken window.

Carlotta opened the door slowly. "I'm so sorry," she sniffled.

"It's okay."

I saw the relief in Carlotta's blue eyes. I held out the bags I'd filled. "I brought a few things with me," I said. "I hope you don't mind."

Carlotta looked into the bags filled with food, clothes, shoes and even a couple pairs of earrings. "Mind?" she said. "How can I ever thank you?"

Then she grabbed me and squeezed so tightly I thought she'd never let go. "And these are for you," she said, dropping the angel earrings into my hand. "When I saw those earrings, I thought I needed guardian angels more than you did. I just didn't realize that I already had one . . . you!"

Katy S. Duffield

Kid Samaritans

No act of kindness, no matter how small, is ever wasted.

Aesop, *The Lion and the Mouse*

When I was eight years old, my family and I lived in a rough, old, two-bedroom house. There were nine of us: my parents, my two brothers, two sisters, a step-brother and step-sister—all in all, we were a crowded and lively bunch.

On one hot, summer day we noticed a frail-looking woman walking down the road in front of our house. The old lady was pale and thin, and she was wearing a simple blue cotton dress and old, beat-up brown shoes.

She walked by our house every day. My brother Kirby and I started to pay closer attention and noticed that as the woman walked, she looked at the ground and examined the dirt as if she were searching for something. She was so thin, we wondered if she had anything to eat. We were sure that the blue dress was all she had to wear. With so many kids in our family, we didn't have much—but compared to her, we had a lot.

Our hearts ached for the old woman, and we wanted to help. Kirby and I got the rest of the gang together, and we made a plan. We rummaged through our piggy banks and collected all of our quarters, dimes, nickels and pennies. Then we told Mom about our plan to help the old woman. Not only did she agree with our generosity, but she helped out by adding some dollar bills to our stash of money!

Even though the old woman was poor, it seemed to us kids that she carried herself with dignity. We didn't want it to be obvious that we were just *giving* money to her. Our plan was to place the money—a little at a time—on the side of the road where the old woman usually walked.

Just before her usual time to walk past our house, Kirby and I put a handful of coins and a dollar bill on the roadside. Then we ran and hid in the house. We watched as the old lady approached the area where we had left the money. When she saw it, she seemed a little hesitant at first and looked around, a little confused. Then, turning in our direction, she smiled and bent over to pick up what we had left for her.

We all giggled with delight knowing that we had just made her day brighter.

For many days to follow, as the old woman walked

by our house, she picked up the money we left for her. She would look over her shoulder toward our old, stone house and wave "thank-you" toward us. We would wave back, hoping that she really didn't know what we were up to.

For the remaining summers that we lived in that old house, we continued to put coins on the roadside, convincing each other that she never knew who her kid Samaritans were.

Karen L. Landrum

Reprinted by permission of Zander/Jacobs Media, Inc.

The Secret Pals

We secure our friends not by accepting favors, but by doing them.

Thucydides

May sunshine glittered on my desk as I thought of how time had flown by. It had been a wonderful year even though I had changed schools, had to make all new friends, have new teachers and ride the bus to school. Although at first I had been a bit scared, I had made it through.

I really liked my homeroom teacher, Mrs. Sims. And best of all, I had made a new best friend, Amity. Amity and I did everything together. I had never had such a fun friend.

One day, Amity and I were sitting at lunch talking about a girl named Susan who was in another home-room. Susan was big for her age, and her clothes were out of style. She just looked like she really needed a friend. So we thought of a plan that might help Susan feel better. Amity and I decided we would be her secret pals.

We began it all with a greeting card in her desk. While Susan was away at math class in another room, we asked Mr. Byrd, Susan's teacher, to put it into her desk. Another day, we left her some cookies. For about two weeks we secretly left things for her, like a note with some candy and once even a balloon.

In the lunchroom one day, Susan told us all about what she had been finding in her desk. She asked us if we knew anything about the gifts. We innocently shook our heads, saying that we thought it was all really cool, though.

When Amity and I got back to our classroom, we broke into giggles—then we shared with Mrs. Sims what we had been doing. She smiled and said she was happy that we had shared our secret with her.

The day before school was going to end for the year, Amity and I planned the final surprise for our secret pal. We went to the principal's office, and he asked over the loudspeaker for Susan to please come to his office. We waited, smiling from ear to ear. On the principal's desk we had put some flowers and a card for our friend.

Susan was nervous as she came into the principal's office, but her face broke into smiles when she saw us standing there next to the card and the flowers.

"You were the ones all along!" she whispered, with tears in her eyes.

As I climbed the step into the school bus at the end of that day, I smiled to myself. It had been a better year than I would ever have imagined. I had made lots of new friends and enjoyed my classes, but best of all I had made someone else's year a little brighter.

Carla Reimche

Miss Feather's Lesson

Kindness is a language which the deaf can hear and the blind can see.

Mark Twain

After school one day, I saw some boys poking a stick into a thorn bush and laughing. My worst fears were realized when I heard a faint "meow" from inside the bush. I ran over and grabbed the stick away from them and peered into the bush. There I saw the most pitiful kitten I'd ever seen. Her color was questionable because of the dirt and blood matted into her coat. The thorns of the bush were pushing into her little body, and she was crying with pain. I *had* to get her out of there.

Crawling carefully into the bush, I freed her from the entangling thorn branches. My arms got totally covered in scratches—not just from the thorns, but from her claws as well, as the frightened kitten tried to hold on to me.

When I got home, I called out, "Mom! See what followed me home!" My mother was used to me bringing home stray animals. This kitten would be no different—she would have a home if she wanted to stay with us.

After carefully removing thorns, cleaning wounds and bathing this poor creature, I found that I had a beautiful, snow-white, long-haired kitten with sky-blue eyes. Because of her silky coat, I called her "Miss Feather."

The following week, a new family moved into our neighborhood. They had a daughter named Judy Ann. Judy Ann talked "funny"—funny to the kids in our neighborhood, anyway—and they laughed at her. I felt sorry for Judy. I protected her from the kids who were mean to her, and we became friends. Judy Ann adored Miss Feather as much as I did and helped me to take care of her.

One morning at breakfast, Mother said, "Molly, why don't you give Miss Feather to Judy Ann? She has no cats of her own—and you have so many!"

"But, Mom, I found Miss Feather!"

"You just think about it."

That night I lay in bed and thought, and thought and thought. I decided that it *would* be a good idea to give Miss Feather to Judy Ann. She lived just two doors down, and I could still play with Miss Feather whenever I wanted. Once I had made my decision, I couldn't wait for morning to come so I could tell Judy Ann about it.

Judy Ann was thrilled to tears! We hugged and hugged as I passed the purring kitten to her.

Most pure white cats with blue eyes are deaf, and Miss Feather was no exception. Because little Miss Feather couldn't hear, she required constant and faithful care. Judy Ann was the perfect mistress for her—no one would ever understand Miss Feather's needs as completely as Judy Ann. Do you know why? Because Judy Ann was also deaf.

Molly Lemmons

My Brother's Gift

Last Christmas, when I was in the fourth grade and my brother was in the first grade, our school held its annual Holiday Shop. At the Holiday Shop students can purchase things like necklaces, keychains, bracelets, hair clips and other small items for their friends and family as Christmas gifts.

Since my brother really wanted to participate, my mom gave him $2.00 to buy his Christmas gifts. He was very excited because he had picked out a special necklace that he wanted to buy for her.

When he got home from the Holiday Shop that day, he couldn't wait to show it to me. He pulled out a green box with white tissue paper inside and opened it. A gold chain with a little red flower and a pretend diamond next to gold letters that spelled out, "Grandmother," was inside.

"Wow," I said. "It's beautiful."

Since my brother was in first grade and was just learning to read, he didn't realize that the necklace said *"Grandmother"* instead of *"Mother."* I didn't want to hurt his feelings by telling him that he had bought the wrong necklace, so I didn't say anything. My brother ran and put the necklace under his bed to hide it from Mom until Christmas morning.

I didn't know what to do. I knew that on Christmas morning, when he found out he had bought the wrong necklace, he would be very upset. So I did what any good big sister would do.

When he wasn't looking, I snuck the necklace out from under his bed and put it in my backpack. The next day I took it back to school and asked the woman who ran the Holiday Shop if I could exchange it for the *"Mother"* necklace. She said yes. When I got home that day, I put the necklace under my brother's bed, exactly where the other one had been.

When my mom opened it up on Christmas morning, my brother was so thrilled! My mom's eyes filled with joy. (My mom knew what had happened, which made the necklace even more special to her!) I knew I had done the right thing.

My brother still does not know what I did, but I'm positive he will hear about it in twenty years or so!

Emily J. Puffpaff, 10

$\overline{2}$

HONESTY
IS BEST

Truth is the only safe ground to stand on.

Kelsey Lyn Carone

Moms Know Everything

When my mom woke me up on a dark and rainy Wednesday morning, I realized that I felt the same way as the weather—gloomy. I was in first grade, and I had a spelling quiz later that day, my first quiz ever.

Did I really know all the words? Or was I clueless? I wasn't planning on finding out. The night before, I schemed what I thought was a perfect plan, one that was sure to fool both of my parents.

As I sleepily opened my eyes, I let out a horrific groan. "Mommy," I whined, "my stomach hurts." I groaned once again to make sure that my mom believed what I said.

"Do you have a stomachache?" my mother kindly asked, and I nodded with yet another moan. "Does it hurt anywhere else, honey?" my mother questioned me again, feeling my forehead.

"No, not right now," I replied.

My mother took my temperature as my father leaned over me with concern in his eyes. I was usually a very healthy child and up-to-date on all my shots, so my parents pondered what could be wrong. The thermometer beeped, revealing that I did not have a fever. My mom looked from the thermometer to me—and back again to the thermometer. I knew something clicked in her head. She knew that I had a spelling quiz that day as she had been helping me to practice my words. The thermometer signaled that I was okay, and I looked as healthy as ever.

With a twinkle in her eye, my mom instructed me to lift up my shirt so she could examine my tummy.

Just some stomach prodding, and I'll be on my way to skipping school and that dreadful quiz, I thought. My mother gently poked my stomach and made some knowing noises, "Hmm, umm, yes, yes."

I couldn't take it any longer! I let out a yelp of laughter and was soon rolling around screaming with giggles as my mother proceeded to tickle me some more. When I settled down, everyone knew my cover was blown and that I was not sick. I desperately insisted that I was in agony, and then, knowing that it was useless, started begging to stay home. My parents refused, and slowly I got dressed and ready for school.

Later that day I found out that spelling quizzes aren't really that bad. Since then, I have never again tried to fake being sick. I know that it is nearly impossible to fool my mom—a pediatrician—into believing that I am sick when I'm not.

After all . . . moms know everything.

Emily Rider-Longmaid, 13

Oops, I Messed Up

The other day at school we had an assembly. When a speaker is talking, we are supposed to be quiet and listen—that's what I usually do. But this time I kept talking to my friend Jamie. My teacher got up and walked around, trying to figure out who was talking, so I looked innocent and kept quiet until Mrs. Nussbaum gave up and sat down.

Then I started again. What I didn't see was that our P. E. teacher was sitting two rows ahead of me. She got up and came over to tell me to behave and listen, and then she went back to her seat.

After the assembly, my teacher asked me if I had gotten into trouble with the P. E. teacher. "Not me," I answered. "It must have been someone else."

She looked at me and said, "It's a good thing it wasn't you, or you wouldn't be having recess." Then she excused our class and sent us outside. I thought I was off the hook until we came back into the building. My teacher and the P. E. teacher were talking to each other, and they were looking my way.

When we went into the room, Mrs. Nussbaum told our class that we had some thinking to do. She said "someone" had caused a disturbance at the assembly, and until she found out who it was, none of us would be having any more recesses. When some of my class-mates pointed to me, Mrs. Nussbaum said she had already asked me, and that I had said it wasn't me. She said that I wouldn't have any reason to lie. She was looking right at me in kind of a funny way when she said that, and then she turned away.

Jamie looked at me and said, "You started it. Why don't you admit it?"

"Because then she'll call home, and I'll be in lots of trouble and probably not be able to go to my soccer game tonight."

"So we all have to suffer because of you? That's not fair."

"Did you want to say something, Jamie?" Mrs. Nussbaum asked.

He looked at me. I wasn't sure if he was going to turn me in or not. "No, nothing," he answered while he glared at me.

After school, I waited until everyone had gone. I walked home slowly, thinking about what I had done. Why did I have to talk when I wasn't supposed to? Worse yet, why couldn't I just admit it when I was wrong? Now I had gotten the whole class into trouble.

I went into the house and stood by the kitchen

door, knowing what I had to do. I walked in and saw Dad.

"Hi, son. Your mom is running late, so I've started supper. We'll eat early so we can all go to your soccer game. You'd better change."

I looked at Dad.

"What's wrong?" he asked.

I told him the whole story. He said we had to call Mrs. Nussbaum right away. Dad called the school and had Mrs. Nussbaum paged. When she came to the phone, he handed the receiver to me.

"I have to talk to her?"

"Yes, you do."

I took the phone and told her it was me, that I was the bad kid. She said I wasn't a bad kid; I just had messed up. In the end, I had been honest. She wasn't even going to punish me!

When I got off the phone, Dad said, "I'm proud that you finally admitted what you had done, but I think it's sad that Mrs. Nussbaum almost had to punish the entire class for your misbehavior."

"Does that mean I can't go to soccer?"

"That's up to you. You decide if you think you deserve to go to the game."

I looked at Dad and knew the answer. "I'll call my coach and tell him I won't be there."

When my mom and big brother came home later, they asked why we weren't going to soccer. My dad looked at me, and I explained it all.

"Wow," my brother said.

"What?" I asked.

"Well, I think it's great you told the truth, even when you knew it would make you miss the soccer game."

I like my big brother, and I look up to him. I thought he was only proud of me for the scores I make in my soccer games. Now I realize he could be proud of me for being honest.

That night, my brother helped me write a letter apologizing to Mrs. Nussbaum and the class. Even though I was nervous to go to school, I knew what I had to do. The next day in class, I was shaking as I read from my paper in the front of the classroom. When I finished, I didn't know what to expect. Some of the kids were upset with me, and I don't blame them. But others came up to me and thanked me for being honest.

I try not to talk during assemblies anymore, but let's face it—no one's perfect—least of all me. But now, when I do something wrong, I admit it. Life is just way simpler that way.

Mike Schneider as told to Nance Schneider

Reprinted by permission of Zander/Jacobs Media, Inc.

Vitamins

You must give some time to your fellow men. Even if it's a little thing, do something for others—something for which you get no pay, but the privilege of doing it.

Albert Schweitzer

I was in my room getting ready for school when Mom stormed in with an angry face cemented in place. *Ooh, scary. Watch out, world!* As she stared at me, I mentally ran down a list of all the things I could have possibly done wrong that she could have found out about.

"We had a deal," she seethed through her teeth, pointing at me. I cocked my head to the side and frowned.

"I don't know what you're talking about."

"I'm talking about the green and white vitamins I just found in the toilet."

Shocked, I slowly shook my head. I hadn't done that since I got caught. "I don't know how they got there, but I swear, I didn't do it."

Okay, here's the thing: I hate taking vitamins. They're nasty. I gag when I try to swallow them, and then I taste them for the rest of the day. The very smell makes the bile rise in the back of my throat. They're chalky, then slimy as they start to dissolve in my mouth. My cheeks soon puff out with water, causing me panic every single time. I have to fight to calm down enough to swallow. Sometimes it takes three tries to get them down.

Jen, who's only nine, thinks it's so funny when Mom yells at me for "making a scene." I can't stand that smug look she gets. She loves telling on me when I spit them out. One day I'm going to spit them right at her.

Terri thinks it's all a big game. She likes to pretend she's choking and then bust up laughing. As the baby of the family, she acts like the whole world revolves around her, and everything is done for her entertainment.

But Dad's a health-nut, and so we have to go through this every morning. For awhile, I was good at pretending to swallow those nasty green and white pills. When no one was watching, I'd stick them in a pocket. Then at the first chance, I'd flush them down the toilet. If I threw them in the trash, someone might see them. Pretty smart, huh?

One morning, Mom caught me slipping the

vitamins into my jean pocket. She was pretty cool about it, which was surprising. We talked it out and agreed I only had to take one pill instead of all three. That I could deal with. I took my one vitamin as promised from then on.

"You're grounded for this, young lady."

I dropped my jaw and stared at her. "But I didn't do it," I wailed. "Honest, I didn't."

She came back with, "So they just got there by magic."

"I don't know." I plopped on my bed, bewildered. I had no clue what was going on. *It has to be Jen or Terri because I didn't do it. Why is it that they can get away with anything? I can't because I'm "the oldest and have to set a good example for the girls." Not fair at all. Why isn't she grilling them? I've been choking down those nasty things just like I'd promised.*

Mom looked at me suspiciously. "If you lie to me, you're grounded for an additional three weeks."

"I'm not lying!" I wiped the tears from my cheeks with the back of my hand.

"Jennifer! Terri!" She called my sisters into the room. *Great, now they can watch her humiliate me.*

Jen wandered in with Terri skipping not far behind. I glared at them, scanning for guilt. Terri had her normal life-is-wonderful face. There were no in-betweens with her. She was either happy as can be or yelling her head off. *If she is guilty and doesn't 'fess up, I'll make sure that smile is gone. Baby or not, I am not going to get grounded for something she did.*

Jen was missing the smug smile. I expected her to rub this in my face for days. She didn't choke on the vitamins. *Wait a minute . . . did she set this up on purpose?* Rage growled in my chest. I squinted my eyes at her, daring her to smile at her cleverness. All I got back was a shrug. *Hmmm.*

"Do you know anything about these pills being in the toilet?" They both looked up innocently and shook their heads. I couldn't believe it. I didn't do it, so one of them had to have done it. And I was going to pay.

"This is so not fair," I said, the anger rising in my voice.

"Don't you take that tone with me," Mom warned. "You admit it right now, or you're grounded for four weeks. I will not tolerate lying."

I stared at her, stunned.

"I'm not lying," I shouted at her. "I've been swallowing those stupid vitamins every day. I don't know who put those pills in the toilet, but I didn't."

She shook her head at me. "You leave me no choice. Four weeks."

"It's not fair!" I started crying again and buried my face in my pillow.

"I did it," a tiny voice said.

I looked up cautiously. Mom spun around. Jen was looking at her feet, digging her toe in the carpet. She looked up at me, tears in her eyes.

There was something about her face that hit me deep. I groaned inwardly.

"I didn't mean for you to get in trouble. I just can't stand those pills either."

Everyone just froze there silently. Finally, Mom turned toward me and sighed.

"I'm sorry I didn't believe you. But that's what happens when you disobey in the first place," she added.

"You," she pointed to Jen, "to your room. We need to talk."

Jen looked at me, chewing on her lower lip. "I really am sorry." The guilt filled her voice as she turned, and they all left my room.

I let out a big sigh and flopped back on my bed. I stared at the ceiling as the emotion slowly drained away. I wanted to be angry with her, but I couldn't. She was my little sister. Besides, she'll be cleaning toilets for a month and getting lectured by Mom. I think that was punishment enough.

Maybe all that fuss at the table was to cover her vanishing trick with the pills. Maybe we had more in common than I thought. I smiled.

Jaime Johnson

What Goes Up Must Come Down

The Fourth of July picnic was one of the most exciting things that happened each year in my neighborhood. No kid wanted to miss the chance to win first prize in the bike-decorating contest or to eat fried chicken, watermelon and brownies all day long.

But the best part was the fireworks display that capped off the night.

Each year, the fathers took their sons to pick out the latest and greatest fireworks. The boys were always excited to show off what they had picked out, and everyone couldn't wait for it to get dark.

The year that I was six, the boys surprised all of us kids with sparklers. I remember being fascinated with them as they sizzled in my hand.

Some of the older kids weren't as easily entertained. To make things more thrilling, they began to throw their lit sparklers. As I watched the streaks of fire soar through the dark night, simply holding the sparkler was no longer enough for me either. I had to join in the excitement. And so I threw my sparkler.

Unfortunately, I didn't throw mine in the same direction as the other kids. Nor did I have the good aim that they did. No sooner had the sparkler left my hand than it had landed on the arm of one of our neighbors, Mr. Miller. Before I could do anything about it, Mr. Miller was on fire!

Thankfully, the adults who were near him were able to put out the fire right away. I realized I had made a terrible mistake, but I wasn't ready to admit to it. I quickly walked toward the tables of food and began eating some watermelon.

Staying at the picnic was tough. I couldn't wait to go home, but I also knew that leaving before the fire-works show would look weird. After all, I had been looking forward to it for days. But as each colorful burst lit up the night sky, I was just glad that the show was that much closer to being over.

When my family got home that night, I headed straight to my room, put on my nightgown and climbed into bed. That's when the tears started streaming down my face. Normally, I slept with my door open, but that night I closed it because I was afraid someone might hear how upset I was.

A few minutes after I had crawled into bed, I heard a knock on my door. I was still so upset that I couldn't even utter the words, "Come in." My dad opened the door, realized I was crying and sat down next to me.

I don't think he even had a chance to ask what was wrong before I blurted out, "Dad, I'm the one who set

Mr. Miller on fire!" Then I sobbed even more.

My dad looked disappointed, but not angry. "Well, honey, I'm glad you told me." After a pause, he added, "I think you already know why what you did was wrong. But we need to make it right. Tomorrow, we will get Mr. Miller a new shirt. We'll take it to him and make sure that he is doing okay. And you can tell him that you are sorry for what you did."

I felt better because I had told my dad, but I was not looking forward to talking with Mr. Miller. He had always seemed a little grumpy to me. I couldn't imagine that he was going to be any nicer after what I did.

I remember picking out a shirt with my father the next night and going to Mr. Miller's home. As he listened to me say how sorry I was, he was neither friendly nor as angry as he could have been. He accepted the shirt with gratitude, and his actions made me feel that he had forgiven me.

When my dad and I headed home that night, I knew that I had done the right thing. Mr. Miller deserved to know who had hurt him and to receive an apology. The other kids deserved for me to step forward, too, so people would know for sure that they hadn't done it.

Telling the truth certainly hadn't been easy. In fact, seeing Mr. Miller at the picnic each year never became comfortable. But it beat holding a secret inside that was bigger than I was.

Kathleen Whitman Plucker

Start with the Truth

When in doubt, tell the truth.

Mark Twain

It was a beautiful sunny day, and Mary and I were playing in her new basement because it was so hot outside. The two of us were best friends, so we naturally did what best friends do—we did everything together. We went camping together, we trusted each other, and always stuck up for each other.

But that day, something changed.

I'll never forget the look on Mary's face when she knocked over her mother's favorite vase that was on the table. The flowers and vase crashed to the floor, and the vase cracked into tons of tiny little pieces. I looked at Mary and said, "There's no way to fix this!"

Mary burst into tears. "What am I going to do? What am I going to say?" She looked at me while she wiped her tears and asked, "Can you say that you did it?"

I was shocked. I didn't know what to do or say, and I started to pace back and forth.

"Okay, I'll do it," I said.

That very second, her mother came downstairs to ask about the loud noise she had just heard. Mary said, "Mom, we were sitting on the couch, and Michelle put her feet on the table and knocked over the vase."

Her mother looked at me and shook her head. "I don't know how many times I have to tell you girls, you don't put your feet on the table."

I apologized to Mary's mother and told her I would buy her a new vase. She said not to worry, but just be more careful. I felt so bad—and I didn't even do it! I know that I had kept Mary out of trouble, but I also felt that it wasn't right.

I didn't go over to Mary's for a few days, and she didn't come to my house, either. I was busy cleaning and doing extra chores. Finally, I earned enough money to buy Mary's mother a new vase. I shopped around for a vase that looked like the one that Mary had broken until I found one that I thought her mom would like. Wanting to get it over with, I went straight to Mary's house to give her mom the new vase. When Mary saw the vase that I had worked so hard to buy, she burst into tears again.

"Mom, I have to tell you something. I broke the vase, not Michelle," she confessed. "I asked her to take the blame for me."

Mary and I looked at each other with relief. Now I

knew that Mary felt it was wrong to lie about the vase, too. Mary's mother had a talk with us about the importance of telling the truth from the beginning. Then Mary decided that she should do something to make things right with her mother and me. She asked if she would take us to the store where Mary picked out some beautiful flowers for her mom's new vase and a pretty friendship bracelet for me. And she paid for them herself with her allowance.

Michelle Rossi

Spelling Bees

Real integrity is doing the right thing, knowing that nobody's going to know whether you did it or not.

Oprah Winfrey

I was the best speller in my third-grade class. Everyone knew it. I could spell difficult words like "precarious" and "amendment" without batting an eye. Perfect scores beamed up at me after each weekly spelling test.

Our teacher Mrs. Brown's rule for spelling tests was that if you didn't get at least 60 percent correct, you had to copy each word for next week's spelling test fifty times. Ryan, the kid who sat next to me, was not what you would call the sharpest tool in the shed. He struggled for C's in every subject, including spelling. On Thursday, when Mrs. Brown passed back our spelling tests, I sneaked a glance at Ryan's paper and saw bold red marks glaring back at him—56 percent. He quickly folded the paper and stuffed it into his desk.

By the next Thursday I was so confident in my spelling abilities, I had decided that I didn't need to study for our spelling test. As Mrs. Brown slowly mouthed each word and then repeated it, the silence was broken only by furious pencil scratching until Mrs. Brown spoke again.

"Handkerchief."

As I rapidly put pencil to paper, I stopped. My mind was racing as I scribbled h-a-n-d-k-e-r-c-h . . . *now what? "I" came before "E," except after "C"—right? But this isn't true all the time.* What if this is one of those exceptions? My mind was blank—I needed to think quickly.

Mrs. Brown started to move on to the next word. Then it hit me. *Ryan knows how to spell it! He wrote these words fifty times each—there's* no way *he would forget them.* Ryan had put his pencil down, and it was a wide-open road between my eyes and the word that I knew he had correctly written on his paper. My eyes rolled to the right. There it was, spelled out in Ryan's scrawling handwriting. My eyes went quickly back to my own paper, and I finished the word with the letters "i-e-f."

I remained tense and nervous as Mrs. Brown read the last spelling words. My stomach was in knots, and my mind was racing. *I had just cheated—for the first time in my life. Was this the way I wanted to keep my perfect* record—*by being a cheater?* I snapped out of it just as Mrs. Brown told us to pass the tests to the front. Frantically, I erased what I had written earlier and replaced it with what I knew was the wrong answer. "e-i-f," I wrote.

As my sweaty hands released my pencil and passed the test up to the front, I heaved a big sigh of relief. I held my head high as I passed my less-than-perfect test to the front of the room. So what if my perfect scores were no longer intact?

At least my honesty was.

Alyse Cleaver

Stand Up and Stand Tall

Just as we sat down for lunch at our desks, our teacher, Sister Joanne, announced that she needed to step out of the classroom for a few minutes. She instructed the class to eat in silence while she was gone, and said that those who didn't would have to answer to her when she returned. It was well known that Sister Joanne was tough, and her punishments were even tougher. So we had to be on our best behavior.

Sister Joanne hadn't been gone for ten seconds before the classroom started to buzz with chatter. From one corner of the room I heard Josh ask Nick, "Trade ya my Ho-Ho for your Twinkie?" At the other end of the room I heard Samantha tell Kayla, "Let's sit together on the bus for the museum field trip tomorrow."

And so it went all around me, until the buzz was at full volume.

After awhile, I, too, forgot about Sister Joanne's

instructions, leaned across my desk and asked Liza, "Can I have some of your Smarties?"

At that very instant, as soon as the words were out of my mouth, Sister Joanne walked into the room. The return to silence was immediate. You could have heard a pin drop. Sister Joanne slowly looked around the room and said, "If you were talking while I was gone, then please stand up."

The guilt weighed heavily upon me as I slowly stood up, dreading the punishment that awaited me. Worse, I felt all alone when I realized that I was the only one in the classroom standing. The shock at my classmates' dishonesty turned to confusion and then to disappointment!

I could see the room of people before me, but I couldn't bear to look anyone in the eyes. I stood alone for what seemed like forever, but was probably less than a minute as Sister Joanne continued to look around the room with her knowing eyes. Then she simply said, "Karen, you may sit down now," and returned to the front of the classroom.

No punishment followed. Nothing.

That experience gave me the courage to be honest, even when it's difficult, the importance of taking responsibility for my actions, and the confidence to stand up for what was right, even if I stood alone.

Oh, and I also learned that Sister Joanne may have been tough, but she was also equally fair and compassionate.

Karen V. Lombard

Herbie, Come Home

My best friend, Karen, had a parakeet named Herbie who was loved and cherished by all. His constant singing always put everyone in a good mood even on sad days. Most summer mornings, Karen would set Herbie's cage out on their back patio. Herbie loved looking at all the other birds flying in the air.

As usual, on a warm, summer day, Herbie was sitting in the morning sun in his cage on the patio. Karen was inside her house eating her breakfast, and I was sitting on their patio watching Herbie while I waited for her to finish.

"Hi, Herbie. How are you today?" I asked.

He answered me in his sweet singing voice as if he knew what I was saying. I got up from my chair and walked over to his cage. I noticed his water bowl had tipped over and that water had spilled over into the bottom of the cage. I decided to open the cage door and take out the bowl so I could refill it for him. The minute my hand went in the cage, Herbie flew out. He was nowhere in sight!

"Karen, Karen, please come out here!" I cried.

"What is it?" she replied, as she ran out. I didn't have to answer—she saw the empty cage.

"How did Herbie get out?" Karen wailed.

"I don't know! Maybe the latch on the cage door was broken," I replied. I tried to keep the guilt I was feeling out of my voice. I was nervous and scared, especially when Karen started crying.

"What is it, Karen?" her mom asked.

"Oh, Mom, Herbie is gone!" she cried. Mrs. Hanick took us both in her arms as we all looked skyward for Herbie. Then she suggested that we get busy and make some posters to hang up around the neighborhood.

"LOST BIRD. Small green parakeet that answers to the name Herbie. Family desperately misses him," read our signs. We must have hung a dozen or more posters as we went up and down the street calling his name. Still nothing. Days turned into weeks, and still no sightings of Herbie. The whole time I was feeling guilty about the secret I was keeping from my best friend.

After a month had passed, I had to tell *someone*. I finally confessed to my parents what I had done. They agreed that I had to tell Karen the truth.

"The longer you keep this secret, the more it will hurt your friendship," my mom said. I agreed. I already had been trying to avoid Karen, and she couldn't understand my new behavior.

I went to my bedroom and opened my piggy bank that was full of quarters and dimes that I had been saving for Christmas presents. I spilled all the coins onto the floor and counted my money. I had $12.50. I asked my dad if he would drive me over to the pet shop.

"I have to fix this, Dad," I said. I could tell by the smile on his face that he knew what I was talking about.

As we parked in front of the store, I saw a parakeet that looked almost identical to Herbie in the pet-shop window. He even had a small yellow patch on his head just like Herbie's.

"That's him," I told Dad. When we went into the store, the pet-shop owner told me that the bird was $15.00. My dad gave me the extra money that I needed. The pet-store owner put the bird into a paper bag with holes in it and handed it to me. I couldn't wait to get home and take Karen her present.

When I knocked at her door, I handed her the bag and told her to be careful. She gently opened the top of the bag and looked in.

Karen shouted with glee. "It's Herbie!"

"Well, not exactly," I said.

"But it has to be him! He has a yellow spot on his head identical to Herbie's."

"Karen, there's something important that I must tell you. It was my fault that Herbie got away. I accidentally let him escape. His water bowl was upside down, and I was trying to help, so I opened the cage door to refill the water dish for him. Before I knew it, he was gone. Oh, Karen, I'm so sorry . . . will you ever forgive me?"

Karen looked at me with tears in her eyes.

"I'm glad you told me the truth," she said. "You're my best friend! Of course I forgive you. Besides, you did a good job of picking out Herbie the Second! Come on—let's show him his new home."

Being honest about Herbie's escape had made me feel better, but having Karen forgive me gave me the greatest feeling of relief I have ever had.

Terri Meehan

3

HAVING
COURAGE

It's better to be a lion for a day than a sheep for all your life.

Sister Elizabeth Kenny

Help! The Adventures of
a Scaredy-Cat Girl

Only when we are no longer afraid do we begin to live.

Edith Wharton

"Wow, I can't believe you're sleeping out in a tent," said my brother Michael. "You were so scared that night at your Girl Scout camp."

I lifted my chin. "That was different. I was only nine then, and that Girl Scout camp was in the deep, scary woods. Tonight we'll be right in Brittie's backyard. It's all fenced in."

"So you girls think you'll be safe then," he said, grinning.

"Cut it out!" I snapped. "I'm learning how to be brave from Brittie because she camps out all the time. She even rides horses!"

"I'll be praying for you," Mike teased.

"Hey, girl," Brittie said with excitement when I arrived. "We have tons of snacks in the cooler."

"I brought my flashlight," I said, trying to look brave.

Brittie's tent was set up near the back fence. When it got dark, we got on our pajamas, lit our flashlights and climbed into our sleeping bags. After a few hours of snacking and chatting, Brittie fell asleep. Suddenly, I felt alone. I heard owls hooting and other strange sounds that hadn't been there when Brittie was awake.

"I don't like this," I whispered softly. But then I reminded myself that I was brave enough to be here. And no bears were here like I'd imagined at Girl Scout camp. No deer, no moose, no raccoons . . .

I closed my eyes and snuggled into my pillow. I was just starting to feel calm when I heard voices. I shot up, terrified. Whatever they were saying was in a language unlike anything I'd ever heard. I could not understand one word!

My heart raced, and I could hardly speak. "Brit?" I managed to whisper. "Hey, wake up. There's something out there."

"HUH?!" Brittie rolled over in her sleep.

"You have to wake up because . . . just listen! Listen to the voices outside, really close to our tent!"

Brittie jolted awake, and we both listened. "That's a language from another planet," she assured me.

"That's what I thought!" I said. "That means we're surrounded by . . . *aliens!*"

We both shivered. "We have to escape," I said, trying to act brave.

"We'll make a run for the house," Brittie said.

"Yeah, and we'll throw snacks at them to distract them," I added.

"Good plan!" Brittie said.

I felt proud. "Get ready," I said. "Now unzip the tent." We did. "Let's run for it. Now!" We bolted from the tent, throwing the snacks behind us into the darkness without looking.

"Aliens! Aliens! Help!" we shrieked, racing into the house and up the stairs to wake up Brittie's dad. Her dad came stumbling out of his bedroom, looking sleepy and worried.

"Dad! This is for real. There are aliens from another planet out there!"

"We just barely escaped," I added.

Brittie's dad looked as if he were trying not to laugh. "I guess I'd better find out about this then," he said. "Let me borrow one of those flashlights." Before he could go outside, the phone rang.

"It must be them," I warned. "They're after us . . . don't answer that telephone!" But he did answer it, and we saw him smiling as he listened.

"Yes, everything's fine," he said to someone. "The girls just became very frightened . . . they were camping out right near the fence." Who in the world was he talking to?

"No problem," Brittie's dad said at last. "Thanks for calling, and I'm sorry for all the noise."

"What, Dad? What!?!" demanded Brittie.

Her dad smiled and yawned. "That language you heard? The people next door have some visitors from another country."

"They do?" Brittie asked.

"Yes. They were out by the fence, studying the stars."

Brittie and I gaped at each other. Talk about embarrassed!

"You probably scared them just as much as they scared you," he laughed.

"Sorry we woke you," I said.

Then I looked at Brittie and said, "Let's try camping again!"

So we climbed back into the tent, ready to get a good night's sleep. *Hmmm*, I thought. *We had a real adventure! And I was pretty brave after all. Yeah, no more Miss Scaredy-Cat for me! Wait until I tell Michael!*

Grace Presnick, 10, as told to Eileen M. Hehl

Saving Mom

When I was eight years old, my life changed. Up until that frightening day, everything was normal—I went to school, had fun with my friends and did all of the ordinary things that an eight-year-old does.

One night, while I was at home with my mom, she started choking on her steak dinner. She was coughing and coughing, trying to get the piece of meat up, and she looked like she was panicking. My mom looked up at me with a scared look on her face—then she passed out.

I was freaking out! I asked myself, *What should I do?* Since Mom and I live all alone, there was no one else to help. Something told me that if I didn't do something IMMEDIATELY, I wouldn't have my mom anymore.

So I grabbed her and did what I remembered about the Heimlich Maneuver. My mom is in the medical profession, and we had talked about this life-saving process before. I had also seen it on a television show.

Mom had always told me that you need to know about stuff like that because you never know when something will happen. I wasn't sure that I was doing it correctly, but I guess I did a pretty good job because Mom came back to consciousness. I had moved the piece of steak that was stuck in her throat enough so that my mom could start breathing again. I had just saved my mom's life!

Mom told me to call our neighbor, who came right over. Our neighbor called 911. I didn't let go of my mom and was crying until the ambulance arrived and the paramedics started taking care of her. I was so relieved that they were there! The meat was still stuck in her throat, so my mom had to go to the hospital. Mom asked if I could ride in the ambulance with her, so they let me. Even though I knew that she wasn't going to die anymore, I wasn't ready to let her out of my sight for even one second.

People always say, "It will never happen to me," whatever it is. But it can—and this proves it. Every adult and child should learn the Heimlich Maneuver because you never know when you will need it. *Everyone* needs to know how important it is.

After that day, it seemed like everyone at school had heard what happened. My teachers told me how proud of me they were. The local newspaper interviewed both me and my mom, and they published a story about it. Mom started calling me her "angel."

My mom and I have always been really close because it's always been just the two of us, but this has brought us even closer. Ever since that night, I have felt like smiling because she did not die. I am so thankful to God for giving her a second chance at life. To me, she is the best mom ever.

Some of my friends said that it was bravery that made me do the Heimlich Maneuver on my mom to save her life, but I think it was something different.

It was love.

Laura Ann Lee, 11

[EDITORS' NOTE: *For more information about the Heimlich Maneuver, go to www.heimlichinstitute.org/ howtodo.html.*]

My Dad, My Hero

Courage is being scared to death—but saddling up anyway.

John Wayne

It was just another morning, like any other. My dad ate his English muffin, drank his coffee, then kissed my mom, my sister and me good-bye. "You never know if we'll see each other again," he would always say. Dressed in his gray suit, he walked in the warm spring air to his bus stop on the corner.

The same as always, he rode the bus to the town where he caught the subway and bought a newspaper from a stand outside the train station. Taking his usual spot along the platform, he folded his paper for the ride.

Then he heard someone scream, "Oh, no!" A lot of people were trying to see over the edge to the track below. At first, he kept to himself, wanting to stay in line for his train. But the cries grew louder, and he had to know what was going on. So he tucked his paper under his arm and walked over to the group. When he reached the edge of the crowd, he looked over and saw that there was a woman lying on the tracks. *Why isn't anyone doing anything? Why are they just standing here?* he thought. Frowning, he put a hand on the edge of the platform and hopped down. He approached the woman and bent over her. She was breathing!

Not wasting a second, he scooped her into his arms. The crowd got ready to help him. Several people reached down to take the woman. Just as he handed her up, he heard a loud rumbling. He looked down the track to his left, and his breath caught in his throat. He was staring into the headlight of an oncoming train!

He quickly grabbed the edge of the platform. He felt himself being lifted up just as the train pulled in. Shaking, he looked around. His head was pounding. Several people were trying to care for the woman while others ran for help. He was sure the woman was now out of danger. Not knowing what else to do, he straightened his tie and boarded the train for his office.

"A funny thing happened on the way to work this morning," he began as he carefully cut his pork chop that night. And, in a matter-of-fact tone, he told us about what happened that morning.

"I can't believe that no one was doing anything!" I said.

"Well," said my father, glad to have the opportunity to repeat one of his favorite sayings, "that just proves that you can't follow the crowd—you have to think for yourself."

"Daddy," said my sister, "you saved that lady's life!"

"Yeah, Dad," I said, "and you could have been killed." He shrugged.

My sister and I looked at each other. We were so proud. What he had done was so brave! "I'll bet this will be on the news tonight!" I said. We jumped up from the table and ran to the living room.

But there was no report of the event on TV. We checked the local paper in the morning, expecting a front-page story. But there was nothing there either.

I never heard what became of that woman. I like to think that she went on to do something really special with her life. But what matters most is that her life went on, thanks to my dad—my hero.

Moira Rose Donohue

Life Is Precious

When I was five, I was diagnosed with leukemia. I did not feel really bad like other people with leukemia, though. I knew what it was, but I also knew I could beat it.

My parents and I first knew something was wrong when I started to develop a large bump on my thigh. We went to see what it was at Bloomington Hospital, and they were talking about just cutting it out! But when they took a blood test, it was not right, so they tested it again. It still was not right, so they took my blood to the lab for more tests. When the results came back, the doctors told my parents and me that I had leukemia.

We went home and packed clothes and all the stuff we would need for the hospital trip. We went to Riley Hospital in Indianapolis and stayed there while they checked me and poked me with needles like I was a pin cushion! Later, the doctors put a port in my chest, which is a thing that helps them take my blood. I got to go home again with a lot of medicine.

One night, I woke up in the middle of the night and saw a little girl with wings floating above my toy shelf. I knew then that God was taking care of me.

The whole time this was going on, my dad had cancer, too. Then, when I was six, he died. I felt terrible, but I knew he was out of his pain.

Once when I was in the hospital, I got to shake Muhammad Ali's hand! So it has not been all bad.

I made a best friend who also had leukemia at the same time that I did. Boys usually have it longer than girls do, so he has had it longer than I have had it. We would see each other now and then when my leukemia was gone. Now his has come back. I visit him a lot and miss him. I hope he gets better.

It took a long time, but this is my third year in remission. Once my leukemia was completely gone, they took out the port. I was really glad about that.

I have learned that life is a very precious thing, and that it is important not to waste it.

Caitlin Conley, 11

"I'm Going to Call Your Mother" Brothers

Keep your fears to yourself, but share your courage with others.

Robert Louis Stevenson

I spotted the three of them out of the corner of my eye. It was the "I'm Going to Call Your Mother" brothers. We called them that because everyone—our school principal, the crossing guard, the nice lady at the candy store—literally everyone, was always threatening to call the mother of the wild eleven-, ten- and eight-year-old brothers.

It was a hot afternoon in late summer, and Barbara, my younger sister, and I set up a lemonade stand in front of our house. We set the picnic table at the curb, covered it with a pretty tablecloth and were in business. We had only had one customer so far and were checking the street for any new traffic when we spotted the boys.

With long side-glances, the boys passed on the opposite sidewalk. We could see they were sizing up the situation, but the big question was . . . for what?

"Oh, no . . ." said Barbara as she spotted them.

"Ignore them," I said, not taking my eyes off of them.

"Should I get Mom?" asked Barbara in a whisper.

"No, just ignore them!" I snapped.

Barbara rushed off in search of Mom anyway, and I was alone.

At the far corner, the boys crossed the street. They were now on my side of the street and heading toward me.

At ten years old, I was a neighborhood tomboy. At our school relay races, I had outrun the oldest of the three brothers. I figured that there might be trouble when the rest of the boys teased him for losing to a girl.

The boys slowed down a couple of houses away. Then it happened in such a fast instant that it seemed to move in slow motion. All at once, they bolted toward me and flipped over the picnic table. I watched in horror as Mom's favorite glass pitcher flew high into the air, streaming lemonade all over me. Everyone froze; all eyes were glued on the spinning pitcher.

I was the first to break the spell. My arm shot up and somehow caught the handle of the pitcher in mid-air. The boys stood defiantly.

"Why don't you go call your mommy?" they teased.

Without even thinking, I thumped the pitcher down to safety, stared the oldest boy right in the eyes and *growled*. Not something *like* a growl, or *sort* of a growl; I bellowed out a growl that started in the pit of my stomach, gained momentum somewhere in my chest and exploded out of my mouth. The boys paled at the sound of it.

"Run!" they shouted to each other.

I took off after them. The thought suddenly crossed my mind that it was three against one, and if any of them could actually count that high, I would be in big trouble. What the three of them did figure out was that while not outnumbered, they were outspirited. They cut through a neighbor's yard, jumped a fence and ran off.

I watched in disbelief as they scurried to safety. If I had had the energy, I would have thrown up my arms in victory and danced a jig, but I couldn't quite figure out what the victory was that I had just won. I sat down, panting, on the nearest lawn to catch my breath and figure it out.

Then it hit me. In my anger, I had never doubted that I could catch all three—and so, that's how I had acted. And because they could see that I *believed* that I *could* catch them all, they had hightailed it out of there. Somehow thinking I could do something, and putting all my energy into only that possibility, had made it happen. Bravery? Self-confidence? Call it what you will, but it was mine for the keeping.

As the shadows got longer and the late afternoon

heat began to release its grip on the day, I walked slowly home, head held high. The "I'm Going to Call Your Mother" brothers were in for *quite* a summer.

JoAnn Palombo

My Big Sister

I think a hero is an ordinary individual who finds strength to persevere and endure in spite of overwhelming obstacles.

Christopher Reeve

My big sister Katie was born with a tumor in her head. When she was nine, she had to have an operation. After her surgery, Katie was frightened and stuck to Mom like a leech. She was having a hard time in school and couldn't concentrate very well. One day, her teacher's aide, Mrs. Guppy, who is also a figure-skating coach, called and said, "Maybe Katie should try skating." She thought it would be good for Katie.

My mom said, "Sure."

So Katie started to skate. Her main goal was to know that she could control her own body. Little did we know that she would have a bigger goal come to her.

After she had skated for about three years, she entered her first competition. All of her teachers and friends were there. That day she won two medals! She was so happy that she yelled and screamed when she got home that night. She wore her medals to school the next day and showed all of her friends and teachers.

The following year, there was a big carnival show at the end of the season. Mom and Grandma sewed a beautiful costume for Katie. The night before the show, something happened. Katie got sick again. She didn't come out of the hospital until the day after the show. Katie was really disappointed that she didn't get to wear her dress, and she also felt like she had let down her club.

The next year Katie ended up in the hospital again. She had to have her blood tested four times a day and had to watch everything she ate.

This time, Mom called Mrs. Guppy. "I think Katie should try skating again."

Mrs. Guppy said, "Sure, I'd love to be her coach again."

Katie competed in the Jean Norman Competition, which is one of the three biggest skating competitions in Saskatchewan, where she placed first *and* second. The best part was that she got to wear the beautiful dress she thought she'd never get to wear—the one that Mom and Grandma had made for her for the carnival show.

After all that, she was asked to try out for the Saskatchewan Team. She started training after school twice a week. About a month before the big tryout, she trained four times a week and worked really hard.

The night before the tryout, Katie told us that she was going to make the team, no matter what. I think that she was really nervous. When at last she stepped out onto the ice, she skated the best program that she could skate. The marks were posted, and Katie had come in first. She made the team!

Katie didn't make the team all on her own. She had lots of people who helped her. Mom drove Katie and Mrs. Guppy to competitions; Dad gave money; Ellen, my other sister, and I cheered her on. The most important person was Mrs. Guppy, her coach. Katie used to be scared to use her own body or to do almost anything on her own. Thanks to Mrs. Guppy's help, Katie isn't afraid anymore.

My sister is special. Her goal was to compete in the Special Olympics Canada Winter Games. Katie had to go all the way to New Brunswick for that event, and she had to go without Mom. She skated her best and WON the silver medal in the Ladies' Special Olympic Level Two Figure Skating.

Katie is a champion and my hero!

Lauren Durant, 10

A Life Saved

It was one of those summer days. We couldn't stand the heat, so it seemed like a good idea to go to the beach. My oldest brother, Michael, agreed to take my younger sister, Lisa, and I to Lake Michigan for the day.

We drove with the windows down and the radio blasting. I sat in the front, and the wind saved me from the heat as it blew through my hair. We parked near a beach we had never been to, but it didn't matter because I love the beach—any beach!

As soon as we carried all our things down to the sand, I ran to the water and stood there, letting the waves wash over my feet. Then I dove in and swam while the water rushed over my body. It felt icy cold at first, but it didn't matter because the sun was scalding hot.

The waves were big and powerful that day. I wasn't the best swimmer because I had taught myself to swim, but I thought I could swim pretty well. Soon

Michael and Lisa joined me, and we had a lot of fun together. When Michael got out of the water, Lisa and I continued to jump the waves, and slowly we drifted further away from the beach.

Suddenly, it got hard to swim back toward the shore. As I began to struggle, I saw Lisa's face just above the water. The waves were crashing over her head, and she was screaming when she wasn't swallowing water. I tried to swim quickly to her, knowing that I had to be my fastest or she could drown. Finally, I got close enough to grab her. I stopped swimming and tried to put my foot down, but I couldn't reach the bottom. That's when I really began to panic.

When Lisa grabbed onto me with all her life, I began to see that I couldn't support her because I didn't know how to tread water, let alone be a lifeguard. We were both flapping our arms, trying to stay on top. The next thing I knew, we were underwater, and it looked like the end.

I remember wondering if anyone had seen us go under. A TV show of someone drowning flashed through my mind. *Would that be us?* I resurfaced once more and screamed with terror. Finally, Michael heard us. He went running toward the water, dove in and swam to us. I felt his hand reach out and grab my body. Then I looked up and saw that he had Lisa under his other arm. We were saved!

When we made it back onto the beach, Lisa began coughing up water. My whole body ached, and I felt like I'd just run a long race. I saw a man behind

Michael who had also come to help us, but Michael had gotten to us first. I reached up and kissed Michael on the cheek and told him I loved him. I meant it more than ever. Lisa and I were both crying, but happy to be safe.

I love and care about life so much more now. I am so grateful to be alive. I look up to Michael as my hero. And I decided to play more with Lisa, no matter how busy I might be.

And I decided something else: I signed up for some swimming lessons and learned how to tread water. Then, as soon as I could, I taught Lisa how to tread water, too.

Rachel A. Maddix, 14

The Wrong School Bus

I took the bus home after school every day in the first grade. I never had a problem with the bus driver, the kids that I rode with or getting home from school that year. But when I was in the second grade, I had a ride I'll never forget.

At the end of the second day of school, I stood staring at the long line of shiny yellow buses. They all seemed really big to me, and they all looked the same. Suddenly, I couldn't remember which one was mine. I bit my lip, trying to think of my bus number. I was afraid if I didn't hurry, they'd all leave without me. Finally, I remembered that yesterday my bus had been parked second in line.

I quickly climbed aboard, but as soon as I sat down and looked around, I realized I'd made a mistake. I didn't know anyone sitting in the smooth, red seats. Where was Emily? Justin? The bus pulled away and started down the road. *Wait a minute!* I thought. *Stop! Something's wrong!* I got a sick feeling in my stomach, kind of like when it's really dark at night and you hear a strange noise.

The bus bumped along, and the farther it went, the worse I felt. When I looked out the window, I couldn't tell where I was. But I was sure of one thing: I wasn't headed home. That's when I got really scared.

At the first stop, I got up and walked to the bus driver. He had big, hairy arms and was wearing a green cap. "I think I'm on the wrong bus," I whispered to him.

"Wrong bus?" he said in a loud voice. "Then you have to get out here." He stared at me and pointed toward the open door.

I knew that I was never supposed to walk alone in the city, but I also had been taught to obey adults. The bus driver told me to get out, so I climbed down the steps, and the bus pulled away. Another boy and a girl had gotten off the bus and ran into a house, but I stood on the sidewalk all alone.

A big, busy street was in front of me. I felt like my house was on the other side of the street. *I'm old enough to cross alone,* I thought. I just had never done it. I looked both ways. When no cars were coming, I rushed to the other side. Safely on the other side, I started walking up a hill. *Where should I go? Should I go to a house and ask for help? Should I take a ride from a safe-looking person in a car?* Something inside told me to just keep walking up the hill.

What if I stay lost? I thought, and I felt myself begin to shake. I knew I was too big to cry, but I couldn't help it. My mom always told me that God would keep me safe, so I tried my best not to be scared.

Finally, after walking a few blocks, I saw some houses that I was sure I'd seen before. Then I saw a street sign for Third Street. I lived on Fourth Street! I knew that my house couldn't be too far away. When I turned the corner, there was my mom walking down the street toward me. I was so happy to see her that I ran into her arms!

She hugged me tightly, and at last, I felt safe.

"Here you are, Kate! I was so worried when you didn't get off at the bus stop!" We walked the rest of the way together. I was so glad to see my house.

Later, I learned that the bus driver had been wrong to let me off where he did. He should have made sure that I got home safely. I didn't know that sometimes adults make mistakes, too. And after talking about what happened, my mom and dad said that I could have followed the boy and girl who had gotten off at the same stop and asked to use the phone at their house. Since they went to my school, they would have been a safe choice to ask for help.

I found that it wasn't easy facing something so scary. But it was a little easier when I knew that my mom and dad were looking out for me. And you know, I think that God was, too.

Kate E. Frezon, 7, as told to Margaret S. Frezon

4

EVERYONE IS SPECIAL

I am just a person,
The way all people are,
In the very same way
That the sun is just a star.
Deep down inside I'm special
Just like the awesome sun,
But it's not just me that's special,
It's me and everyone!

Chrissy Booth, 10

Two Best Friends

The lightning bugs flickered in the night sky, competing with the Fourth of July fireworks. All of the other kids from our block were down at the ballfield watching the rockets and spinners on the ground. I sat next to Paul, in our neighbor's yard, watching the sky burst with colors. Both of us were waving sparklers as fast as we could.

"I wish I were a lightning bug," said Paul.

"Why?" I replied. "They're so tiny, and you're big."

"'Cause they're free. They can go wherever they want."

Paul was the very best friend any six-year-old could have. We did everything together—watched TV, ate Popsicles, studied how the birds build their nests and guessed what shapes the clouds made. But our friendship was different than other boy/girl friendships. Paul couldn't run the bases in Little League games or play on his bike with the other boys in our neighborhood. He had something wrong with his hip, and he couldn't walk. Paul was confined to a wheelchair and had to wear a V-shaped leg brace 24/7. Since he couldn't play with the boys, he played with me—the girl next door.

I never really understood exactly what was wrong with his hip, but if he tried to walk on it without the brace, his leg bone would rub against the hip bone, and they would crumble. He told me that if he didn't wear this brace and stay in the wheelchair for two years, he would never be able to walk again at all.

So every day when school was in session, I would carry his books as well as my own back and forth to school. Paul sat in the first desk in the first row near the door so the teacher could park his wheelchair in front of his aisle. If he had to go to the bathroom, we had to help him get into his wheelchair, and one of the boys would go with him to the bathroom to help him. If he lost his balance, he would fall backwards and get hurt. The braces didn't stop Paul from learning, though; he was really smart in school. He just couldn't be active like the other boys. Paul's legs got really skinny over those two years, but the day finally came when he could take off the brace. He walked, but he walked funny, sort of a hop-walk. His one leg, the one that had the bad hip, was shorter than his other leg, and he walked on his tip-toes to make up the difference.

We still were best friends even after the brace came off. Only now we got to play some stuff outside, as long as they were things that Paul could do without straining his leg. We ate lunch at each other's houses and watched videos in the basement. He still didn't play with the boys, but I never thought about it or wondered why. I just figured it was because he'd rather play with me. After all, I was his best friend.

We were best friends until his family moved away when we were ten. I'll never forget the special times we had during those years. Paul's disability taught me to be more accepting of those who cannot always do for themselves. Because of him, I know that they're not that different from you or me.

Gayle Krause

The Birthday Helper

Sometimes when we are generous in small, barely detectable ways, it can change some- one else's life forever.

Margaret Cho

I was so excited as I walked into the classroom. Today was my birthday! I set down the box of treats I had brought for the class. Mom and I had baked all last evening making cupcakes and icing them. I wanted them to be just perfect.

Birthdays were a big deal in our classroom. The birthday person brought a treat for the class, and he or she got to choose someone our teacher called "the birthday helper" to pass them out. My friends, Andrea, Crystal and I had already talked about choosing each other on our birthdays.

I still hadn't decided which of my two best friends I was going to choose. I knew that both of them were expecting me to pick them, but I just couldn't decide. I didn't want either one of them to be mad at me.

A loud shout interrupted my thoughts. "Hi, April!" yelled Lisa.

No one liked Lisa very much. She had dirty blonde hair that looked like it always needed to be brushed and often wore rumpled clothes. The kids made fun of her a lot. She annoyed me sometimes, too, but I tried to be nice to her.

"Did you bring treats today?"

"Yes," I answered. "Today is my birthday!"

The bell rang, and we quickly went to our seats. Our teacher, Mrs. Doughty, started class, and I glanced at Lisa.

Lisa's parents were divorced, and her dad gave Lisa and her mom a lot of problems. I found her crying in the bathroom one day, and she told me that her dad had threatened to kidnap her. Her mom started dropping her off at school every morning, and a teacher walked Lisa from the building to her mom's car after school. My friends said they pitied Lisa, but my feelings went deeper than feeling sorry for her. Lisa once told me that I was the only friend she had. At times I felt embarrassed to hang out with her, but she never seemed to notice when I didn't want her around—at least, she never said anything.

I pushed aside my thoughts as I reached for my spelling paper. The rest of the morning flew by, and soon we were dismissed for recess. My two friends immediately pounced on me.

"Who are you choosing to be your helper this afternoon?" asked Andrea.

"I'm not sure yet," I said, feeling uncomfortable.

"You should pick me. We've been friends longer than you and Crystal. Will you pick me?"

Before I could answer, Crystal jogged over to us.

"Let's play on the swings!" she suggested.

The three of us ran for the swings, but Crystal pulled me back slightly. "Who are you picking to be your birthday helper?" she whispered.

My stomach twisted. *Why were they making this so hard for me?*

"I'm not sure."

"What do you mean? You promised you were going to pick me!" stated Crystal.

I looked down. "I'll see."

I escaped making a decision during the rest of recess. No matter what I did, I couldn't win. If I picked Andrea, Crystal would be mad. If I chose Crystal, Andrea would feel that I liked Crystal better than her. There didn't seem to be a solution. I walked back to class with a heavy heart.

An hour after recess, Mrs. Doughty announced that today was my birthday. I stuck a smile on my face when everyone sang "Happy Birthday," but my stomach felt like I had just eaten raw liver. I retrieved my cupcakes at the back of the room and slowly went to stand beside Mrs. Doughty.

Indecision paralyzed me. I didn't know what to do! Should I choose Andrea or Crystal?

Andrea stared right at me. I got the message: *You'd*

better pick me or else! I bit my lip.

Then Lisa caught my attention.

"No one ever chooses me on their birthday!" she said in her loud voice. Her face looked so sad. I saw the hurt and pain she felt from the rejection she constantly faced from our classmates. Suddenly, I knew my decision. I stopped biting my lip, and peace settled over me.

"April, who will be your birthday helper?" asked Mrs. Doughty.

With total confidence, I said, "Lisa."

Lisa's head shot up, and her eyes were as wide as quarters. She stared at me, her mouth hanging open.

"Really?" she barely whispered.

I smiled brightly and nodded. Lisa scrambled out of her seat and rushed to my side. She looked so proud to stand beside me as we passed out the treats. Her face practically glowed.

I felt Andrea's angry glare from across the room. Crystal ignored me. I knew they were mad, but it didn't dent my happiness. Today was my birthday, and I knew I had done the right thing.

Just before I rushed out to catch the bus at the end of the day, Lisa stopped me. Her face still radiated with joy. She flung her arms around my neck and hugged me.

"April, you are the best friend I've ever had!"

All I could do was smile and hug her back. I felt so good inside! As I watched Lisa skip down the hall, happiness filled my heart. This had turned out to be a wonderful birthday after all.

April Stier

William aka Bill

Kind words do not cost much. Yet they accomplish much.

Blaise Pascal

William was a bully. He moved to our town during the fourth grade from no one knew where, and I wished he would just go back.

William sat in front of me in class, and sometimes when I went to the front of the classroom, he would stick out his foot to trip me. I freaked out every time I had to go up to the front. Even if William didn't end up doing anything to me, he would sit there grinning, his crew-cut hair bristling with pleasure at my tension.

On the first day of fifth grade, William showed up in a stained sweatshirt with his typical Cheshire-cat smile. William's name came right after mine alphabetically, and when our new teacher—a 6'5" giant the kids called "Mr. Sandy"—took the first attendance, he boomed out my name, and then . . . "Bill."

William looked startled.

"Bill??"

"His name is William!" a classmate called out with disgust.

Mr. Sandy looked at William, who was slouched down in his seat.

"Is your name William?"

"Yeah."

"Do you like being called William or Bill?"

"I *hate* William."

"Bill." Mr. Sandy uttered it and then continued calling the attendance.

During the first weeks, Mr. Sandy asked Bill to pass out papers and take on other duties. He praised Bill's abilities and called on him in class, coaxing answers out of him. Soon, he didn't have to coax, and Bill was raising his hand with the rest of us. Mr. Sandy didn't treat Bill like he was a bully—he treated him like he was any other good kid.

Bill was starting to change. My opinion of "Bully William"—a person to be feared and despised—had changed, too. I realized that Bill had probably been mean because he hadn't felt accepted or liked by the rest of us from the beginning.

We started inviting him into our games. He stopped tripping us in the classroom aisles. Mr. Sandy took Bill aside one day and pointed out that he had natural leadership abilities, which could be helpful.

So instead of controlling the playground like a tyrant, Bill became an honorable leader. Bill taught me how to properly swing a baseball bat. When I tripped and fell down on the playground and broke my nose, Bill was instantly at my side with a tissue.

"I know what to do," he said. "I've had a lot of bloody noses."

"Bill's dad hits him," some kids whispered. I don't know how they knew that, but I knew in my heart it was true. My feelings had completely changed toward Bill over the course of two years. I liked him. I respected him, too, for turning his life around.

Bill didn't go on to sixth grade with us. He moved away as suddenly as he had come, and I didn't know where he had gone. I just wished he'd come back.

Tanya C. Sousa

The Measuring Line

As far as I was concerned, everything was great until Aunt Rose came to live with us. "She's very sad and lonely since Uncle Herbie died," my mom told me while she was making the bed in the guestroom.

"Hi, Aunt Rose," I said to her the next day as she moved into the guestroom. My goldfish had died the month before, so I knew how she felt.

"Hi, Small-Fry," she answered.

I guess that to Aunt Rose I seemed small. She was tall like my dad.

Aunt Rose was always buying surprises for everybody, and she gave me a "measuring line." It was a piece of cloth that looked like a big ruler.

"You just tack this piece of cloth to your bedroom wall," Aunt Rose said. "Then we can watch you grow."

I didn't know why that was so important to Aunt Rose. Almost every Friday after school, as soon as I got home, she was waiting for me in my bedroom. I guess she didn't have anything more important to do.

Aunt Rose would have me stand in front of the measuring line. "You didn't grow one bit," she would say, shaking her head. "Too bad, Small-Fry."

Pretty soon I began thinking about being a "Small-Fry." When I played basketball at school, when I climbed a tree, when I looked up at tall buildings, everything seemed so high up . . . except me! All I could think about was growing taller.

I did everything I could to grow. I drank lots of milk. I created a hairstyle where my hair was piled on top of my head. But Aunt Rose always flattened it down when she measured me.

One rainy afternoon, I went up into the attic. I always did that when I needed to think. I found the big box where my mother kept the clothes I had outgrown. When I came downstairs, I was wearing last year's blouse and pants. The sleeves of my blouse and the legs of my pants were too short, and my arms and legs stuck out.

"You sure are growing quickly," my mother said. "You're popping out of your clothes." But that night when Aunt Rose measured me, she just said, "Nothing yet, Small-Fry."

When Aunt Rose left the room, I stared at the measuring line. I didn't want to see it anymore. I ripped it off the wall. Some of the wallpaper came with it. When my mother came into my room to say goodnight, she looked at the wall. "Where's your measuring line?" she asked.

"I don't want that thing," I answered. "I wish Aunt

Rose would go away, too. She always calls me Small-Fry."

"Did you know that my sister used to call me Shrimp?" my mom asked. I looked up at her. She sure didn't look like a shrimp to me. I told her that.

"And you sure don't look like a Small-Fry to me," she said. "You know, Aunt Rose doesn't have enough to do. It's going to take her awhile to get back to being herself again, now that Uncle Herbie is gone." Then my mom hugged me. "You know, it's how tall you feel that's important," she said. "When you understand someone else's feelings, you grow inside."

I stood there after my mom left. I thought about Uncle Herbie and how much Aunt Rose must miss him. I thought about how busy I am and how sad I'd be if I didn't have anything to do. I guessed that the only thing Aunt Rose had to do was measure me.

The next morning, before Aunt Rose woke up, I put the measuring line back on the wall. When Aunt Rose came into my bedroom to measure me, I didn't get angry. Instead, I asked her to play a game of cards with me. We had so much fun and played for so long that Aunt Rose forgot to measure me. And she didn't call me "Small-Fry," not even once during the whole card game.

Later that night, before I went to sleep, I said a special "goodnight" to Aunt Rose. She smiled just the way she used to smile at Uncle Herbie. I felt myself growing inside, feeling taller than ever.

Beth Savitz Laliberte with Harriet May Savitz

The Carriage House

My grandfather lives in a nursing home called the Carriage House. That's where my grandmother goes almost every day to visit him.

When I sleep over at her house, we go to see him, too. There are lots of old people there. When I first started going there, they would see me coming and hold their arms open for a hug, but I would pretend that I didn't see them and hurry upstairs to Grandpa's room. Just thinking about the other people with their wrinkly faces and hands made me shiver.

I felt safe up in my grandpa's room with him, even though he can't walk, talk or do anything for himself. I would tell him all about my life and sometimes give him a kiss. Even if I felt like I needed to go to the bathroom or I wanted to go to the soda machine, I didn't leave the room.

The first time my little brother, Ben, came with my grandmother and me, he looked like he was going to cry. I understood how he felt. I didn't blame him because he'd never been around people who were so different from us.

One day, I asked my mom about the old people. She told me that they can't take care of themselves anymore and need special care from the nurses, so they live there at the nursing home. I thought about that for awhile, trying to imagine not being able to live in my own home anymore and not able to see my family and friends every day. I began to understand how they feel, and I thought, *They must be so lonely when no one visits them.* So I made a decision.

The next time I went with my grandmother to visit my grandpa, I actually hugged the other old people— and it wasn't as scary as I thought it would be.

Now I am getting used to being in my grandpa's new home, and I'm getting to know some of the other people who live there. And now I know that just because they are old doesn't mean that they don't have feelings or deserve to be loved.

Victoria Thornsbury, 8

Adventure from a Stolen Apple

*Love is the only force capable of transform-
ing an enemy into friend.*

Martin Luther King, Jr.

When I was ten years old, I spent the summer at my
grandmother's farm. Even though I was older than all
of my cousins and most of them were boys, we still
hung out together after we did our chores. We would
wander the countryside, picking wild blackberries
and playing together.

There was one very rundown farm that we stayed
away from because my cousins said that a witch lived
there. They called her "Old Lady Green." I had never
seen her, but one day in late August as we were passing near her farmhouse, we saw that she had a lot of
large apples hanging almost over her fence. We
stopped to look at them.

Then my cousin Paul climbed over the fence. He

reached up, grabbed an apple and handed it to me. Just then, I heard a startled gasp. I turned and saw an old lady watching us.

"Old Lady Green! The witch of Knox County!" my cousin yelled. Then he raced back through the waist-high grass and leaped over the tumbled-down fence.

My eyes couldn't leave the eyes of the old lady. *Why*, I thought, *she's going to cry!* She was leaning heavily and painfully on a stumpy, knotty, worn tree branch. Her head was bald in spots, and her white thin hair hung limply around a face that looked like a shrunken apple. Although she looked about a hundred years old, she was only as tall as I was.

I reached out and handed her the apple. A crooked half smile creased her wrinkled face, and I saw that she only had a few teeth.

"Thank you," she rasped. "Why didn't you run away like the boy did? Aren't you afraid of me?"

"Because at my school we are learning about being kind. I want to help you." This was only half true. I felt like running as fast as I could away from her, but I stood my ground.

Then she sat down on a tree stump, laughed and slapped her thigh. "I'm too old and weak to care for my property. I can only reach the low apples, pears and peaches. I have only a few chickens. I don't want 'em scattered. The only way I've been able to save what I have is to scare the lights out of youngsters by pretending to be a witch. Now I've lost my power over you!"

What should I do? I wondered as I stood there. Even

though I was still a little scared of her, I wanted to stay and help her—and I did. I climbed high up to the sweet apples and brought her a bag full of them. I picked green beans from her weedy garden, and washed and snapped them. I dug up some potatoes. Then I searched the grass near the hen house and found some eggs the hens had mislaid.

When I started for home, I found my cousin, my aunt and Grandma almost running down the road to look for me. They seemed very worried. I quickly explained, "She isn't a witch at all! Just a nice old lady who is very weak and can't pick the apples up high, so she chases away people who try to steal the only ones she can reach!"

Now whenever I see an old lady who looks cross because children or dogs are running around her lawn or through her flowers, I remember Old Lady Green who wasn't really mean or a witch, but simply too weak and too poor to replace what others might carelessly destroy.

Rosemary K. Breckler

5

DOING THE RIGHT THING

I think we all have a little voice inside us that will guide us.
It may be God, I don't know.
But I think that if we shut out all the noise and clutter from our lives
and listen to that voice,
it will tell us the right thing to do.

Christopher Reeve

Box Puppies

Nobody made a greater mistake than he who did nothing because he could do only a little.

Edmund Burke

Last fall, our family was on our way back from a weekend in the mountains. My brother and I were riding in the back seat of our car with our two Labrador Retrievers. I was looking out of my window when suddenly I saw a dog standing by itself on the side of the road. I yelled at my dad, and he made a U-turn to go back and see if the dog was all right.

We walked up to this cold, damp, shady spot, and found out there wasn't just one dog—there were three—and they were puppies. Then we discovered another puppy in a box, down below in the ravine. My dad went to rescue that puppy. He said that it looked like it was going to die. The poor little thing wouldn't eat any of the treats we gave it, and it was shivering and shaking.

My mom, dad, brother and I were full of questions. Who had left these puppies here? Why would anyone do such a terrible thing? What were we going to do with these four darling little puppies? We knew that we couldn't just leave them. Since we already had two dogs, we wouldn't be able to keep them either—especially four of them!

My mom went back to the car and got a dry box. We carefully placed the puppies in the box, and my mom held them on her lap as we drove to the nearest fire station. Since it was Sunday, the local animal shelter was closed. Mom and I walked up to the front door of the station and knocked on the door. A fireman opened the door, and we asked him if they would take care of the puppies until Monday and then take them to the local animal shelter. While we were talking to the fireman who had opened the door, four other firemen had started playing with the puppies. One of the puppies was already running around the firehouse. The firemen could tell how worried I was about these darling little things, and they agreed to keep the puppies until the next day.

As we drove down the mountain, I couldn't get my mind off the puppies. I was filled with all kinds of feelings: happiness, anger and sadness—all at the same time. I was so happy that I had seen the first puppy standing all by itself in the shade, but I was also angry at the person who abandoned them in the ravine. I was sad at the thought of those little puppies all by themselves in that cold before we came into their lives to save them. They were so small—they couldn't have been more than four weeks old.

My mom called the animal shelter the next day to make sure that the puppies had survived. She was informed that they were all there, eating and sleeping quite a bit. Even the weakest puppy, the one that we were afraid wasn't going to make it, was perking up with all the food and warmth. We were told that each of the puppies would be adopted for sure, as they were so cute and friendly.

All the puppies ended up being adopted. They won't ever have to go unloved ever again. I still think about the puppies and wonder how they are doing, somewhere out in this world. I will always feel good about how we rescued them. For some special reason I was looking out of the window . . . just at the right time.

Michael Van Gorder, 9

The Biggest Surprise

*Our character is what we do when we think
no one is looking.*

H. Jackson Brown, Jr.

I couldn't take my eyes off the stickers. They were different and totally cool. I wanted them—badly. So I asked my classmate Kristin, "Can I have some of your stickers?"

"No," Kristin snapped. "Tell your mom to buy you some, and then I'll trade you."

Some classmates had shared their stickers with me, but I only wanted the ones Kristin had. Those were the kind that could stick to my bookbag and make me feel popular.

But my mom couldn't get me any stickers, so I was out of luck. She wasn't around much since my little brother had gone into the hospital. She spent her days there helping him get well. My dad would take me to school, and then grown-up friends would watch me until my parents got home. My dad had no clue about where to buy these special stickers. Hurt and unhappy, I watched Kristin put away the stickers.

I missed my mom.

At recess, I saw some classmates trading stickers with the new girl, Josie.

"Come sit by me," Josie called out.

"I've got to get some water," I answered, half smiling.

After stopping by the water fountain, I snuck back to the classroom. *Good, it's empty*, I thought. The room was so quiet that I could hear my heart pounding. Before I knew it, I was at Kristin's desk. I grabbed three sheets of stickers, ran over to my desk and slid them into my bookbag. *Nobody will ever know I was here*, I hoped to myself. That's when I thought I heard footsteps. I froze and listened for a few seconds, but I didn't hear anything else so I went back out to recess.

When we got back to class, I pretended to read while Kristin searched for her missing stickers. She checked the floor, looked through her books and then asked everyone around her about them. Finally, Kristin went to Ms. White, our teacher, to tell her what had happened.

Ms. White nodded to Kristin and whispered something to her. Kristin went back to her seat, still upset.

"Okay, class, we have a little problem," Ms. White said.

The room seemed to be getting hotter. Somehow, I'd expected that because Kristin had so many stickers, she'd never notice that some were gone.

"Some of Kristin's stickers are missing. Has anyone seen them?" Ms. White asked. No one answered. "Very well, I could check each bookbag to see if one of you has stolen them."

Oh, no, I thought, as my heart pounded again.

"But instead I'm going to ask each student to be truthful."

I could not tell the whole class what I had done. If I told the truth, then no one would like me anymore. And now I had some prized stickers, but couldn't stick them on my bookbag or trade them.

"Mary Lou, do you know anything about the stickers?" she asked.

I felt my curly hair bounce as I shook my head. "No, Ms. White." I could feel Kristin staring at me. Ms. White seemed to look sadly at me before moving on. *Was it her footsteps I heard in the hall?* I wondered.

After asking everyone, she said, "Should someone decide to come to me and return the stickers, I won't tell your parents what happened."

Just as school ended, someone from the back of the classroom said, "Ms. White, I know something about Kristin's stickers."

It was Josie. *Was she the one I'd heard by the door? Would she tell on me?*

Kristin's eyes lit up, and she shouted, "Where are they?"

I held my breath as Josie said, "I can't tell you who took them, Kristin, but I think I can get them back to you by tomorrow."

When I got home and opened the book that held the stickers, I found a note that read:

> *I know you took the stickers. If you're sorry, slip them in my bookbag tomorrow (it has a "J" and a big red rose sticker on the front) and I'll return them for you. I won't tell.*
>
> Josie

So it had been her by the door.

The next day at lunch, instead of having Josie do it for me, I returned all the stickers to Kristin's desk. When Kristin found them, she was very happy. Then something surprising happened. When I opened my bookbag after lunch, I found a sheet of beautiful rose stickers inside.

I turned back to see Josie smiling at me.

Mary Lou De Caprio

Responsible Chrissy

"Here you go. Up, up and away," Chrissy hollered, as she pushed her little brother, Russell, on the swing. Russell giggled and kicked his feet. "Higher, higher!" he shouted.

"Okay, hang on. Here you go!" Chrissy leaned forward and gave the swing an extra hard push.

"Help!" Russell screamed. The swing flew so high it seemed it might go flying off into the sky. Russell started to cry just as their mom came running over.

"I'm sorry, Russell," Chrissy said. "I didn't mean to scare you. I guess I pushed a little too hard."

Mom frowned at Chrissy. "A LITTLE too hard? That was *way* too hard, Chrissy. How could you be so irresponsible?"

Irresponsible! Tears filled Chrissy's brown eyes. A week ago, her teacher had told her she was irresponsible for being late to class. And a few days ago her dad had used the word "irresponsible" when he scolded her for not hanging up her clothes.

"I'm sorry, Mom," Chrissy said sadly.

Chrissy turned away and started to walk slowly down the path that wound through the park. That awful word "irresponsible" kept going through Chrissy's head.

Suddenly, Chrissy noticed a little girl toddling across the grass, heading up a small hill. Chrissy looked around for the parent, but there was no one else in sight. Chrissy knew there was a running stream on the other side of that hill.

Chrissy ran as fast as she could. When she reached the child, she stepped in front of her, blocking her from running toward the water. Chrissy picked up the baby and carried her toward the playground, looking frantically for her mother.

"Where's your mommy?" she asked the child, although she thought the toddler was probably too young to talk. She was surprised when the baby pointed toward some apartment buildings on the other side of the fence. Chrissy noticed a small gap in the fence where she might have squeezed through. On the porch of a nearby apartment, Chrissy could see a policeman talking to a young woman who looked upset.

"Is this your baby?" Chrissy called out. The woman and the policeman came running toward the fence. Minutes later, the baby was in her mother's arms.

Just then, Chrissy's mom and her brother Russell came looking for her. The policeman told them that Chrissy had probably saved the child's life.

"That's a very responsible daughter you have there," the policeman said.

Her mom smiled and said, "I'm happy she did the right thing."

The next day, the headline in the newspaper read: RESPONSIBLE NINE-YEAR-OLD GIRL SAVES BABY, with an article about Chrissy.

"We're proud of you," said her dad.

"You really are a responsible young lady," said her mom.

Now Chrissy is on time coming back to class after recess. She almost always remembers to hang up her clothes, and she is careful when she pushes Russell on the swing.

And nobody ever calls her "irresponsible" anymore.

Diana L. James

The Genuine Van Gogh

I used to think that being a hero meant saving a person's life—like rescuing someone from drowning in a pool or pulling someone out of a blazing fire. I even thought a hero was like a high-scoring professional hockey player or a baseball player who hit a grand slam. I found out that I didn't have to do any of those things to be a hero.

All I did was find a lost cat. I didn't think something as simple as returning a lost cat would make me a hero, but in the eyes of Van Gogh's family, it did.

I had seen several posters in our neighborhood offering a fifty-dollar reward for a missing Ragdoll cat. My dog had just died and I was still upset about it, so I knew how terrible the owners must have been feeling to be without their pet.

I was walking home from my friend's house when I saw a cat hiding under a parked car. I thought he looked just like the picture on the posters. I coaxed him out from under the car and started to pet him. I was sure that it was Van Gogh, the missing cat. He began to purr. It was as if he knew I was going to help him. I quickly ran back to grab the poster from the tree, and Van Gogh followed me. I couldn't wait to get home to show him to my mom. I swung open the front door and shouted, "Mom, look! I found the lost cat!"

She called the telephone number on the poster and no one was home, so Van Gogh and I played together. He was really a fun cat. About thirty minutes later, Van Gogh's owners called, and they came to pick him up.

They were so happy that I had found their cat. They were crying and everything! When they started to hand me the fifty-dollar reward, I said, "No, that's okay." I was just glad to see how happy they were to have their cat back.

The following week, Van Gogh's owners wrote a letter to the editor of our local newspaper. The letter was even published—with my name in it! They said that I'm a real hero, and their family is very grateful that I found Van Gogh. Van Gogh can still play with his family thanks to me.

Now I realize that being a hero can mean just going out of your way to help someone. It seemed like a little thing to me, but to the people I helped it was a big thing.

Austin Black, 10, as told to Nancy Mikaelian Madey

What Kaleidoscope Wanted Most

The love we give away is the only love we keep.

Elbert Hubbard

He was beautiful, the turtle I found. His sparkling eyes twinkled like twilight stars. His high, hard shell was round and brown, and splashed with sunny splotches like the designs in my kaleidoscope, so that is what I named him.

I carried him next to my shirt, dripping, up the hill and across the field. When I got Kaleidoscope home, I unwound some wire fencing and stuck it in the ground. I just knew Kaleidoscope would love his outdoor pen! I set him down in it. He wandered around from corner to corner and then tucked himself in before sunset.

Long after dawn the next day, he still wasn't awake. I knocked, but he pulled farther into his shell. I thought, *I know what you want, Kaleidoscope.* I got a pan and filled it with cool water. But after just a short dip, he went back inside his shell again.

Then I figured out what Kaleidoscope wanted. I got a shovel and turned over some fresh, moist earth. Kaleidoscope poked out his nose and sniffed. "I knew that's what you wanted!" I told him. "Earthworms, all wriggly and squiggly." He snatched one quickly in his jaws. But he hid away as soon as he had eaten. And he wouldn't come out again.

The next day, I was sure I knew what Kaleidoscope wanted. I dug up some plants and put them in his pen. He waddled over and nestled under the leafy stems. Then he stayed there all that day. The next morning when I came to see him, he was still there.

I sank down and curled up next to him. "We have to talk," I said. "I don't understand. I've given you everything turtles want, and you just keep getting sadder every day." I picked up Kaleidoscope and looked him straight in the face. His once sparkling star-eyes were now foggy and dull.

I carried him gently next to my shirt, down the hill and across the field. I reached the stream where we had found each other. The stream was bubbling, and the wind was whispering. Kaleidoscope heard them, too. He stretched out his head and sniffed. He shivered and strained and scrambled. I thought he would jump right out of his shell!

Suddenly, I knew what he wanted most. I was glad that I could give it back to him.

I set him firmly on the stony bank. He padded over the mossy rocks and dove headfirst into the swirling stream. He paddled and pawed, bobbing up and down in the gleaming bubbles. Kaleidoscope looked back at me. The stars were sparkling in his eyes again.

I quickly wiped my own eyes so that all he could see was my smile.

Virginia Kroll

Stolen Conscience

The person that loses their conscience has nothing left worth keeping.

Izaak Walton

Last year, my mom tried to tell me that there really is a thing called a "conscience." You know, that little voice in your head that tells you when something you do is wrong? I never really believed her. I thought about hearing a small voice saying, "Brandon don't do this. Brandon, do that." *That's dumb,* I thought.

Then one day, my dad took me shopping, and we went into a toy store. There were lots of things to buy, especially in this one store where they sell collectable Star Wars cards. I really wanted a pack, but my dad said I couldn't have them so I got mad. After my dad left the store, I put the pack that I asked for into my pocket and walked out of the store.

The next day, I had a bad stomachache, and I felt

that I needed to say something or let something out. This is the first time I ever felt this way. I wondered all day if it was my conscience telling me that I did something I shouldn't have done. It was a horrible feeling, as if someone knew what I had done and told me that I was bad. I felt ashamed of myself.

Then that night, I had trouble sleeping. I was thinking scary thoughts about what could go wrong. *What if someone finds out? Will I get kicked out of the store for good? Will I go to jail?* The next day, I asked my mom if someone would feel anything if they did something wrong.

"Yes," my mom answered. "You would feel sort of sick in a way."

I knew I had to confess. So I told my mom what I had done, and she drove me to the store. She gave me money, and I paid for the cards that I stole. I also told the lady who ran the store that I was sorry. She was nice and said that I could come back to the store again.

After I told the truth, I felt better. But I was still embarrassed that I committed a crime, which I never thought I would do in my life. Even today, anytime I think about stealing, I get the shivers and feel just like I did when I stole that pack of cards. I also learned an important lesson during that week: Listen to your head and heart, not your greed.

Brandon Deitrick, 12

Happy Camper

Yesterday I was a dog. Today I'm a dog. To-morrow I'll probably still be a dog. Sigh! There's so little hope for advancement.

Snoopy

Wherever I went, Happy came, too. He was the best dog a kid could ever have. He was black and brown, a mix of who-knows-what, with big eyes and silly, floppy ears. He would follow me to my friend's house down the road, and when I went inside he stayed on the porch until it was time to go home. Happy was my best friend.

We spent our summers at Camp Wihakowi in Vermont, where my mom was the camp nurse. I got to explore nature trails, do arts and crafts, and swim in the chilly lake—all with Happy at my side. He didn't like the water, but sometimes he waded around close to the shore. Then he would flop down under a tree to wait until I came out, dripping and wrinkled like a raisin.

One day a counselor named Annie visited our cabin. "Nurse, I need some supplies for our campout tonight," she said. While my mom packed a first-aid kit, Annie turned to me. "Peggy, do you want to join us?"

I didn't answer at first. I was excited to go camping with the big kids, but also a little scared. At seven years old, I hadn't spent many nights apart from my mother. Although I loved sleeping on a cot in our cabin, I wasn't sure about sleeping on the ground in the woods. And what about the stories some of the counselors told around the campfire? Could it be true that Thumper, a huge, wooden-legged man, really plucked campers right out of their sleeping bags at night?

"Can Happy come, too?" I asked at last.

"Sure," Annie laughed, "good to have a dog for protection."

I packed my flashlight, rolled my sleeping bag and joined the other campers on the hike into the woods. Happy trotted along beside me, sniffing at the grass and fiddlehead ferns. Finally, we reached a small clearing. I helped pitch a lean-to tarp while the others dug a fire pit. Happy sat by the path to keep watch. Every once in a while, his floppy ears perked at a strange squawk or hoot.

We roasted hot dogs over the fire and then finally settled into our sleeping bags. I looked up at the inky sky with millions of stars in it and felt so small. But with Happy beside me, I knew I was safe.

Late in the night, however, I was awakened by a growl, crash, screech! Something had gotten into our

camp! But we were lucky—Happy was there to protect us. Then I smelled it. "Skunk!" Annie cried out.
The other campers woke up and plugged their noses.

"Ewww!"

"Gross!"

Then I heard a mournful sound. "Arrooooo!" It was
a loud, sad howl. I rushed to Happy's side.

He'd been hit. He rolled on the ground and rubbed
his nose with his paws. He cried like a little baby.

"We can't stay here," said Annie. "It smells horrible."
So we packed up all our stuff and hiked back to our
cabins.

"What happened?" my mom said when I returned.

"I'll have to wash Happy in tomato soup," Mom
said after I told her what had happened. "It helps take
away the smell."

I looked down at my dog, his head low and his tail
between his legs. "No, I'll do it," I said. Happy was,
after all, my dog. I poured two cans of thick, red soup
over his sleek body. It squished between my fingers
when I rubbed it around.

Happy had ruined my first campout and had made
everyone have to move back to their cabins. Maybe I
should have been mad at him, but I wasn't. *He was just
doing what dogs do,* I thought as I rinsed his fur. I had
assumed he'd take care of me, but it ended up I had to
take care of him. I guess Happy needed me as much
as I needed him.

Margaret S. Frezon

6

BEING A GOOD FRIEND

*Friends are there for ups and downs,
  never leaving with a frown.
  Always letting you have a head start,
  forever you will be in their heart.
  That's the way a friendship should be.
  Me being there for you
  and you being there for me.*

Jessica Crown, 10

A True Friend

My friend is one . . . who takes me for what I am.

Henry David Thoreau

Makayla and I have always clicked. In kindergarten, we were both very athletic and loved racing against each other. Then during the first grade, Makayla and her family went on a trip. On their way home, a bus hit her family's car. At that moment, my friend Makayla's life changed forever.

She was in the hospital for a long time. Every day I hoped and prayed that Makayla would come back to school. After what seemed like forever, Makayla finally returned. When I saw her, I knew my life would change, too. She was in a wheelchair, paralyzed from the waist down.

From that time on, when it is too wet or too cold for Makayla to go outside during recess, I stay in with Makayla and we play together, just the two of us. We have been in the same classes for the last five years. She is an A+ student who never gets into trouble.

Some people think Makayla should be in the "special" class, but that's just not the case. When people try to treat Makayla like she is helpless, she doesn't get down—she just goes that extra mile to prove them wrong. Makayla can do eleven or more pull-ups, hang on the bar longer than most boys, reach up as far as the tallest girl in school (when she is sitting down) and tons of other things.

Sometimes the classroom is crowded with a lot of kids. If you think that stops Makayla, you had better think again! She will get up out of her wheelchair and use the desks and her strength to get to wherever she wants to go. When she needs to go upstairs, and the elevator is occupied or isn't running, then Makayla will crawl up the steps and have somebody bring the wheelchair upstairs for her.

Every springtime at school, we have a day where our whole school does outdoor activities all day, and we keep track of what we have done on a card. Half of the activities include running, which Makayla can't do. I pair up with Makayla, and she will do whatever activities she can. Then I do my running events. After that, I run Makayla's events for her. At the end of the day, I am extremely tired—but happy—knowing that I helped Makayla fill out her whole card. Makayla stands beside me 150 percent, and I do the same in return.

Sometimes people think Makayla doesn't go through the same things that they go through because she is in a wheelchair. But that's not true. She goes through dealing with crushes, issues with her brothers and sisters, school and everyday stuff that every other girl goes through.

So when you see somebody who is handicapped or different, take the time to get to know them. Who knows . . . they may become your very best friend.

Kelsey Temple, 11

The Cool Club

It takes a great deal of courage to stand up to your enemies, but even more to stand up to your friends.

                                        J. K. Rowling

Almost everyone, at one time or another, experiences the pressure to be popular—to be in the "cool crowd." For me, the pressure to be "cool" started in the second grade. Everyone in our class got along, but suddenly, boys seemed to have cooties and girls broke into small groups. There were popular kids and unpopular kids. Making friends started to become complicated.

I went from having a lot of friends to having none when my family moved to a different neighborhood just before I started second grade, and I started going to a new school.

On the first day of my new school, during lunch, I walked over to three girls sitting at a lunch table and sat down. One of the girls was talking about a movie I had just seen. I listened carefully and pretended like I was part of the conversation. During a pause, I cleared my throat and said, "That was a good movie."

Instantly, all three girls turned toward me. The girl who had been talking looked at me like I had three heads. I wasn't prepared for this.

"Yeah," she replied in a cold voice. Then she turned away and started talking again. None of the girls tried to include me.

Well, she doesn't know me, I reasoned with myself. *None of them do.* I tried to join in a few more times, but I got the same kind of response. The same thing happened with other groups of kids when I tried to join their conversations.

By the end of the week, I had made one friend—an adventurous girl named Laura.

One day at recess, a brown-eyed, fair-skinned girl walked up to Laura and me. She was followed by three other girls. The brown-eyed girl spoke proudly.

"Hi, girls. We were wondering if you would like to join a little club we have—'The Cool Club,' that is."

Laura and I exchanged hopeful glances. We desperately wanted to be part of their group. I had tried to talk to them earlier, and they had completely ignored me. But now, clearly, they had changed their minds about me.

"Would you like to join?" the girl asked.

"Sure," Laura chirped.

"Okay," I replied.

After some talking, I found out that the girl who had invited us to join her club was Tiffany. Her friends were Rachel, Tara and Amy.

Laura and I were both very excited. Finally, we would be popular. All of the girls outside our club would be jealous of us and be sorry that they hadn't been kind to us. We would get invited to everyone's parties, and we would get to decide where we wanted to sit in the lunchroom.

Tiffany looked at her three friends and then said, "You guys do want to join our club, don't you?"

Laura and I nodded.

"Well, we think you guys need to join 'The Geek Club' and get kicked out of it so you can join 'The Cool Club.' We've all done the same thing, right, girls?" she said, motioning toward her friends. They nodded.

"Okay," Laura replied.

I was furious. These girls were making fun of us, and my friend didn't even realize it and was going right along with their evil plan.

"Well, Alison, what do you say?" Tiffany asked. "Will you join 'The Geek Club?'"

"Your club *is* 'The Geek Club!' I exclaimed. "And I'm not joining!" I spun around and stomped away from the group. Laura didn't follow me.

I spent the rest of that recess alone, wondering if I had done the right thing. At the end of recess, Tiffany came up to me.

"We're sorry," Tiffany said. "Do you want to join our club now?"

I thought about it. These girls may be popular, but should I really trust them after they had embarrassed me—not once, but twice?

"No," I replied.

That day I learned an important lesson about friendship. I learned that real friends don't treat you like an outsider or act like they are above you, or "cooler" than you. They also don't trick you into embarrassing yourself. You don't have to wait until friends get used to you. You'll recognize a real friend from the start.

The next day, Laura told me she was sorry and asked if I still wanted to be friends. I told her yes because I knew she meant it. I understood why she had done what she did—we had both wanted to be popular much too badly.

I have made many other real friends since that day, and I choose my friends based on how kind, loyal and trustworthy they are. I never again chose who I want to be friends with based on how popular that person is.

Alison Braneim, 13

J. W.

To love and be loved is to feel the sun from both sides.

David Viscott

I first met him in the second grade. He was standing in the middle of the hall looking scared because people were stopping to stare and point at him. I went up to him to see if I could help him. It turned out that J. W. was a new kid in our school and I found out he was in my class. After J. W. was in our class for a while, we realized he was different; he had autism.

A couple of weeks later, our teacher took our class on a field trip to a park. J. W., his mom, my mom and I were all paired into a group. We held hands as we walked around. After the trip, J. W. and I became fast friends. We were always together.

Then we started third grade. We weren't in the same class, so we were really bummed. I had been his one and only friend and couldn't be there to help him out or stick up for him. That was when the kids began teasing him really badly. I was also teased a lot because he was my friend, but I never cared.

One day, this boy was picking on J. W., and he got really scared. He ran into a classroom, hid under a table, and began crying and yelling for me. The principal, four janitors and almost every teacher in the building was trying to get him to come out from under the table, but he just kept calling my name. I was taken out of class and went to try and help him. The second he saw me, he ran out from under the table and gave me a huge hug.

When fifth grade began, I went searching for J. W., but it turned out that he had moved over summer vacation. He now lives in Michigan, and I have not seen him since the end of fourth grade. I think about him so much, though. And I can't help thinking about all the kids who might be picking on him in his new school. The fact that I can't be there to protect him makes me sad. He often told me that he loved me and that I was the one he was going to marry. I cry when I think about him, but I believe that he will find another friend—just like he found me—and he will be okay.

Alanah Coggins, 12

[EDITORS' NOTE: *For more information about autism, go to* www.autism-society.org/]

The Girl with a Lot of Freckles

If you give your enemy a second chance, she might turn out to be your best friend.

Meghann, 13

My dad and I were watching our rival softball team's pitcher. I felt scared of her—she pitched really fast, had a ton of freckles, and she looked older than me. On the way home, my dad told me that during the next softball season, Kayla, the girl with the freckles, was going to play on our team. Little did I know that she would change my life forever.

The next summer, even though we were on the same team, we didn't become friends. But the following winter, Kayla e-mailed me, and we talked online. We ended up talking about anything and everything. Even though it turned out that she was one year older than me, Kayla and I related to each other in lots of ways. Over that winter, we grew closer.

By the time softball season rolled around again,

Kayla and I were inseparable. Even my dad would get our names confused. We spent endless amounts of time shopping and sharing tons of secrets. For my thirteenth birthday party, I decided that all of my friends, including Kayla, would go shopping together and spend the night at my house.

That day at the mall, all of my other friends decided that they would buy friendship bracelets for each other—and they didn't include me. I got so upset. I was crying, and Kayla came over to comfort me. Then she went up to them and asked, "Why are you being so mean to Cara on her birthday?" They just blew her off.

That night was like a nightmare. Kayla ended up yelling at them for being so inconsiderate, and they yelled back at her. I just sat on my sleeping bag crying. I felt like my old friends were betraying me.

After my birthday, Kayla truly became my best friend. At school, my old friends talked badly about me behind my back, but every night Kayla called me and made me feel better. I really don't know what I would have done without her—she gave me strength when I really needed it.

A couple years have passed, and we are still the best of friends. Kayla and I have been through loads of stuff together. She was there for me when I changed schools, and I was there for her when her dad was sent off to war. She has given me tons of advice and has always listened to my stupid problems—even at three o'clock in the morning! There isn't a day that goes by that I'm not grateful for our friendship and for having Kayla in my life.

Who would have known that the girl with a lot of freckles—a girl that I once feared—would end up being my very best friend.

Cara Mulhall, 13

Reprinted by permission of Zander/Jacobs Media, Inc.

The Gift of Friendship

When you are sick, friends can sometimes be a better medicine than the kind the doctor gives you.

Julie Anne, 12

About two weeks before my tenth birthday, I fell while I was Rollerblading and broke my wrist. I had been planning on having my birthday party at a roller rink, and now I wouldn't even be able to skate at my own party! But because we had sent out the invitations and everything was already planned, we still had to have the party at the roller rink anyway.

On the day of my party, I was standing by the front door of the roller rink greeting my friends while they came in. When one of my friends, Sarah, came in the door, I noticed that she was limping. Sarah told me that she had hurt her leg, and that her parents had told her that she could come to my party anyway if she just took it easy and only skated around the rink one time.

Sarah didn't even skate once during the whole party. All of my other friends were busy, having a great time skating—but Sarah stayed with me the whole time. We talked about all kinds of stuff: school, our teachers, what boys we like and who we think is cute—and we laughed our heads off. Because of Sarah, my party was a lot more fun than I thought it was going to be.

A few weeks later, I saw Sarah's mom at the store, and I asked her if Sarah's leg was better. Her mom looked very surprised, and then she told me that she didn't know what I was talking about. She said that Sarah had never hurt her leg.

It was then that I realized that Sarah had stayed with me at my birthday party just to make me feel better. My true friend, Sarah, gave me the best present of all.

Ashley Russell, 10

A Dog's Love

Jared had looked forward all year to the weeklong canoe trip with his dad and the other scouts. At last, they were on the Current River in Missouri, and despite his leg braces, he felt just like one of the other eleven-year-old boys.

Shortly after lunch, the scouts beached their canoes. They planned to swim across the river to explore a cave tucked behind huge granite boulders on the other side.

Putting on his life jacket, Jared studied the river that ran deep and swift and wide, but not too deep or swift for a boy with good legs. To reach the caves, the other scouts were already swimming upstream and letting the current carry them down. At the last minute, they broke from the current and kicked for the rocks, safely reaching the shore. Jared wanted to follow them.

He unstrapped his leg braces and then waved to his dad, who had let Jared's dog, Rio, off the leash to play in the water. Rio liked the water, and her shiny black coat looked slick as a seal in the sun. His dad waved back.

Jared had gotten Rio earlier that year as a gift from Canine Companions for Independence to help him get around easier. She was trained to be a guide dog, and since he'd had her, he was no longer afraid of being shoved around in the halls at school. Instead, Rio would push against his braces, helping him navigate through the stream of boys and girls. Since she came along, the other kids noticed Jared more because they liked petting Rio. Jared was glad to have her even if Rio was just doing the job she was trained to do.

Now Rio's smart eyes were on him, but Jared's look told her no. She couldn't help him swim the river; she was trained to help on land, but not in the water. Besides, this was something he wanted to do on his own.

Jared waded out and sank down, using his arms to paddle. At first it was just like at home, in his pool, where he'd taught himself to swim without the use of his legs. The water was colder than he'd thought and felt as strong as a giant's arms as it tugged at him.

When he got to the middle, Jared heard the other boys calling to him from the rocks. They didn't seem to be getting any closer. He looked back at his dad, who was getting farther and farther away.

Then he realized that he couldn't swim free of the current!

Jared only had time for one word before the giant's arms twisted him around and yanked him under. *Rio!* Water filled his ears and flushed up his nose. He choked and tried to swim out of the giant's grip. But it was no use. The river carried him away.

Suddenly, Jared slammed into something live and strong and sleek as a seal. It was Rio. She pushed against him, just as she did in the halls at school. She looked at him as if to say, *Why did you come out here without me?*

Jared grabbed onto Rio's fur and, with all her power, Rio pulled him to shore.

Safe on the beach, Rio stood over Jared, panting hard. Shivering, Jared reached up and hugged her neck. She answered with a wag of her tail. At that moment Jared understood that his dog had not just saved his life because it was her job. She'd saved his life because she loved him.

Zu Vincent

7

LIVE AND LEARN

You must learn from the mistakes of others. You can't possibly live long enough to make them all yourself.

Sam Levenson

Lessons in Friendship

Some people support their friends and stick with them, no matter what. Others make friends, but when someone else shows up who is cooler than their friend, they dump their old friend.

This story proves it.

Sayla and I had been friends for a year, ever since the first days of fourth grade. We started playing with each other and found out that we were a lot alike. We did everything best friends do—we had sleepovers, shared secrets, did all kinds of stuff together. We were inseparable. We remained close over summer vacation, but then came fifth grade.

We were in the same class, but this year we sat across the room from each other. We only talked to each other at recess and lunch. Sayla started to become friends with the two girls sitting beside her. I got the feeling that Sayla thought they were "cooler" than me. She began spending her recesses and lunches with them, and hanging out with the "cool" people—people that she said she didn't even like at the beginning of the school year.

Soon, Sayla started acting really mean to me. For instance, when I would tell her that I liked something, she would tell me that she didn't like it. She would smirk and act like whatever I had said, or whatever I had told her I liked, was the lamest thing on Earth.

But to her new friends she would say, "You like that? Cool! I don't really like it, but that's okay. People are different." Or when I'd ask her for something, she'd say no, but if her new friends asked her for the same thing, she'd give it to them without a second thought.

I'd still try to play with Sayla, to talk to her, but she would continually ditch me. When I'd ask her what happened, she'd just say, "Things change," as if she really didn't care. When her other friends weren't around, she was almost normal and sort of nice to me, but she completely ignored me when she was with them.

It hurt. It was hard, but I knew I had to get over it. And thanks to some really good friends that I made this year, I have been able to move on. Sometimes that is the best thing to do—to let go. I miss Sayla, and I wish things could have turned out differently, but I know I can't control anyone else's feelings—only my own.

I learned two really important things from this whole thing—what kind of friends I want to have . . . and what kind of friend I want to be.

Tatiana Eugenia, 10

A Day in Never-Never Land

The summer of my eighth birthday taught me the importance of my mother's words and the strength of a friendship. By mid-July, I was completely bored and looking for some excitement. Every day I rode my bike down to my best friend Jana's house, and she'd join me on whatever adventure we had deemed worthy that day.

On this day, my mother had told me not to leave the house because a big storm was brewing in the north. But as stubborn as I was, I went anyway. Jana's mom told her she couldn't go out either, but like me she disobeyed. Within minutes, we were off to Never-Never Land. Never-Never Land was the name we had given to the old, abandoned train station just beyond the railroad tracks. It was our favorite place to play even though our parents had told us that it was dangerous and not to play there. The building wasn't in the best shape, as it was very old.

The wind was strong, and it made it so hard to ride

our bikes that we had to walk them. We reached the station and went inside. Soon, it began to rain—followed by quarter-sized hail balls—then lightning. We were scared and decided we should try to make it home.

As we started out of the building, I noticed that I had forgotten my sweater. I went back inside to get it, and as I walked up the stairs, one of the stairs broke and I fell through it. I could feel my skin burning, and my leg hurt worse than I'd ever known. I couldn't pull my leg out because it was stuck. I yelled for Jana. She ran back in the door, and I cried out to her to help me. Jana was a lot smaller than me, and even though she tried she could not get my leg free.

"I can't get your leg out! I'll go get your mom—I promise!" Jana cried.

I didn't want her to go because I was scared, and I didn't want to be left alone. But I was hurting so badly that I told her to please hurry, and she left. I wasn't able to move without making my leg hurt worse, so I just prayed, asking God to help Jana make it home and that I'd be okay.

After what seemed like days, I heard my mom hollering for me. I cried out to her, and she came in with some paramedics and they helped to get me free. The whole time they were working to get my leg out, I kept telling my mom that I was sorry. All she said was that she was glad I was okay and that nothing else mattered.

After I got to the hospital, they fixed me up and said

that I was lucky that the step didn't break completely or I would have had more than just a broken leg. They also said that I was lucky to have a friend who was willing to go for help even if it meant that she was going to get herself into trouble. I told them that she was more than a friend—she was like my sister, and our friendship would last forever.

That summer, I learned that when your mother says no, she is only trying to protect you; she is not trying to take away your fun. I also learned that a true friend will stand by you—no matter if it means she will get grounded herself—because that's what friends do. No matter what the situation is, as long as you have a friend like that and the love of your mother, you can make it through anything.

Teresa Hosier

My First Bike

It's always helpful to learn from your mistakes because then your mistakes seem worthwhile.

Garry Marshall

I remember how excited I was the day my dad brought home my very first bike. He pulled into the driveway in the truck he had borrowed from work, with my new red bike in the back. My dad lifted it out of the truck with a great big smile on his face. I did not know how to ride a bike, but I was grinning from ear to ear just thinking about learning.

When my dad got home from work that evening, he began teaching me to ride my red bike. There were training wheels on it so that I could get my balance. I would ride up and down the street, hoping that all my friends could see this wonderful new gift that was given to me.

Once I got the hang of riding, my dad raised one

wheel up so that I could get comfortable with one training wheel not touching the ground. Soon my dad took both training wheels off, and I remember feeling nervous and excited all at the same time.

For a few days, my dad held on to the back of my bike while I would ride. I felt so safe knowing my dad was right behind me. Then one day . . . he let go. I didn't know he had done that until a few minutes later. I was so excited when I realized that I was riding my bike all by myself!

After that day, I went everywhere on my bike. I loved riding, and I loved my bike.

I did have one very bad habit, though. Whenever I came back home even for a few minutes, I would lay my bike down on my neighbor's driveway. My dad told me over and over again not to do this. But because our front door was closer to our neighbor's driveway than our own driveway, I kept leaving it there. I really didn't see why he made such a big deal about it. What could happen by leaving it there instead of on our own property?

Then one day, I found out why. Our neighbor pulled into his driveway and didn't see my bike lying there. My new red bike was crushed. My dad tried hard to fix it, but it was too bent. It was never the same again.

Years later, I learned that my dad paid for that bike by putting five dollars a week on it for many months. We did not have a lot of money back then, but he wanted me to have a bike.

I have a photo in my hallway. It's my favorite one.

I'm smiling, and there beside me is my red bike. It has been a great reminder of my father's love for his little girl. And it has also helped me to become more responsible and take better care of my things.

Jean Verwey

Pelican Watching

One day my father took me fishing with him. I told him that I wasn't ready to use my own fishing pole yet, but he brought two poles anyway. I sat in the boat and watched the sea birds as my father untied the fishing boat from the dock and started up the motor.

"What kind of birds are those funny ones with the tiny heads and fat bodies?" I asked, pointing to two birds not far from us.

My father looked up and said, "They're pelicans."

"The littler one looks angry. It keeps flapping its wings at the big one."

"Hmmm," my father said. "Looks like the big one with the yellow feathers around his eyes is the papa. That little one with the gray and white wing feathers must be his baby. The baby wants to sit with him on his post."

"But he won't let her," I said, as I pointed out how the papa pelican kept pushing the baby pelican off the post.

"Oh, look," my father said. "Papa's gonna dive for a fish. There he goes!"

"Go, Baby Pelican!" I laughed. "She nabbed the post!"

"Not for long," Dad said.

Sure enough, Papa Pelican came up with a fish in his mouth. He flew to his messy post, pushed off Baby Pelican and swallowed his fish.

"That's not fair!" I said. "Papa Pelican should share his post with his baby and give her some of his fish."

"I don't know about that . . ." my father said. We watched Papa Pelican dive two more times, coming up each time to knock his daughter off his post.

"Come on, Dad, let's go," I said. "I've seen enough."

"No, wait," my father insisted. "Just a little longer."

The next time Papa Pelican dove, he came up with a fish, but he didn't take it back to his own post. He put it on another post. Then he flew back to his own post and knocked his daughter off.

"He wants her to go to the other post," my dad said.

Baby Pelican flew around for a moment as if she was confused, but the smell of the fish must have caught her attention because she eventually landed on the other post and swallowed the food.

Papa Pelican dove again, brought up a fish and ate it. Baby Pelican squawked loudly. Papa Pelican dove a couple more times to catch a few more fish for himself. Each time Baby Pelican squawked louder.

"Just get your own fish then, Baby," I yelled to her. "You can do it!"

The fourth time Papa Pelican dove, Baby Pelican copied him. Papa came up with a fish in his mouth. So did Baby Pelican. They both went to their own posts and swallowed their food. Baby Pelican cooed, and Papa Pelican flew close to her so he could touch her with his long beak as if he were kissing her.

"He taught her how to fish!" I gasped.

"Incredible, huh?" my father said. "Watching all that fish-eating has made me hungry. Let's catch some big ones!"

"Yeah!" I agreed.

After a short while, we found a cove where the water was calm. My father put bait on a hook and handed the pole to me.

"No thanks, Dad," I said, pushing the pole back toward him.

"I thought you wanted to fish today," my father said.

"I do," I said. "I just want to do it with my own pole."

My father grinned. "It's about time!" He leaned over, hugged me and messed up my hair. "Do you want to put the worm on, too?" he asked.

I looked at the tub of worms. "Well, actually, I think I'll let you handle that."

The two of us fished side-by-side all afternoon. Each time I caught a fish all by myself, with my own pole, I would cheer. And every time there was cause to cheer, my father would lean over and kiss me on the head.

Donna Getzinger

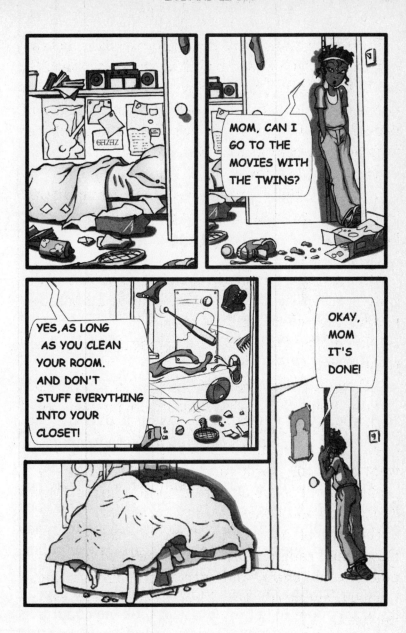

The Purse

In this age, which believes that there is a short cut to everything, the greatest lesson to be learned is that the most difficult way is, in the long run, the easiest.

Henry Miller

My room was a mess. Clothes were all over the bed, on the floor and in my closet. I had sworn to my mom that I'd clean it up, but I'd always have an excuse for not cleaning it. "Busy—can't do it right now," "Have to go to Kristen's house," or "Have to get ready for soccer," were some commonly used ones. No matter what my mom did, she couldn't get me to clean up my room.

So she did something totally unexpected.

I was going to the mall with my friends, and I went up to my room to get my purse. It took me about five minutes to realize that I'd lost it somewhere in the piles and piles of stuff. After another five minutes of looking, I started to panic. So I did the only thing that any girl would do in a situation like this—I called for my mom.

She raced upstairs and asked what was wrong. I told her that I couldn't find my purse, and not only did I need it now because I had to leave right away, but it had over a hundred dollars in it! She suggested that I put some of my things away so that maybe I could see it lying on the ground or something. I started putting some of my clothes away, but my purse still couldn't be seen.

By now, it had been about twenty minutes, and any minute my friends were going to leave without me. My mom told me to clean up more of the clothes so maybe I could find it then. So I did. No luck! Then my mom said to pick up the last bit of clothes, and I would see it.

As soon as I finished cleaning up every speck of clothing, a broad smile spread across her face. I asked her what was so funny. She burst out laughing. I stomped my foot and demanded again that she tell me what was so funny.

As soon as she finished laughing, she said, "Look, Amanda, your room is clean!"

As I looked around my room, I noticed that it actually *was* clean. For one second, I smiled with her, then I asked if she knew where my purse was.

"At the front door, waiting for you," she said. I dashed down the stairs as fast as I could and rushed out to my friends.

My mom was still up in my room, smiling.

Amanda Kelly, 11

This Is for You, Buddy

*Learning by experience often is painful—
and the more it hurts, the more you learn.*

Ralph Banks

"You can buy this bunny for a dollar!" the woman called to us.

My sister, Sharon, and I were heading home from Market Day in town. We had spent most of our money on candy, but we had one dollar left between us.

"A bunny!" I exclaimed. "Let's go see, Sharon!" I skipped over to look at the black–and-white rabbit in the woman's arms.

"We sold all of the other bunnies for five dollars each. He's the last one, so he's a real bargain for only one dollar," the woman said with a smile.

I turned to Sharon. "Come and look at how cute he is. And he's only a dollar!"

Sharon made her way over to me and the bunny.

"He *is* very cute, isn't he? But I don't think Mom and Dad will let us keep him."

"But we'll take care of him," I promised. I had no idea of how to look after a bunny, but I felt sure I would figure it out once we got home. I cupped the bunny into my hands and held him up to my face. He wiggled his nose at me. "Hi, my little buddy. Hey, that's a good name . . . Buddy!" I said excitedly.

Sharon pulled our last dollar out of her pocket, and the woman gave us some food and a small box for Buddy. On the way we talked about what we would tell our parents.

At home, our mother greeted us with a smile. Then she frowned and said, "What's in the box?"

As if on cue, Buddy stuck his little pink nose out of the box to say hello.

"A bunny? Where did you get it?"

"At Market Day, and he was only a dollar! Can we keep him? Please?" we pleaded.

"Oh, I don't know, girls. Your dad will be home from work soon. We'll have to see what he thinks," Mom said.

We took Buddy inside and gave him water and one of my doll blankets for a bed. Then our dad came home, and we heard Mom tell him about Buddy. We crossed our fingers as we heard footsteps coming closer.

"So, you have a bunny, do you?" our dad asked us.

Sharon spoke up. "Yes, Dad, we named him Buddy. We'll take care of him, we promise. We'll do every-thing. Can we keep him?"

"Well, I guess I have a cage to build. He'll have to live outside."

Sharon and I jumped up. "Yaaaah!" we shouted.

Our dad built a cage with a little house and enough room for Buddy to have a little run. Over the summer, we let him out in the garden. Soon it began to get cold outside.

"It's your turn to feed Buddy, Christine," Sharon reminded me one windy and rainy afternoon.

"I don't want to go out there. It's too cold," I complained.

"How do you think Buddy feels?" she said as she went out to feed him. When she came back she said, "Buddy has a runny nose."

"I get runny noses all the time. He'll get better, right?" I asked.

"Hopefully," my sister said.

A few weeks later there was snow on the ground, and we rushed home from school. Sharon stopped at Buddy's cage to shake it, but Buddy didn't come out. Sharon opened the door to his house and noticed that Buddy wasn't moving. I turned to look up at Sharon. She had tears running down her cheeks.

"Is he dead?" I whispered. Sharon could only nod her head.

Later that evening, we buried Buddy in our backyard. We wrapped my old doll blanket around him and put him in a shoebox. We each said a few words about Buddy and then good-bye. I stayed outside after my dad and sister went in. I needed to talk to Buddy alone.

"I made a promise, but I didn't keep looking after you. I'm sorry, Buddy. I'm very, very sorry."

It was then that I learned that it took a lot of work to care for a pet. As the years went by, we had other animals that I helped to look after, and I made sure that no matter what, I did my part. Every time I didn't feel like helping, I would do it anyway, and I would say to myself, *This is for you, Buddy.*

Christine Middleton

The Power of Attitude

People forget how fast you did a job—but they remember how well you did it.

Howard Newton

I strongly believe that your outlook on life has a lot to do with whether or not you will succeed. A very wise man once told me, "Life is an attitude." During the summer that I turned nine, I learned that lesson firsthand.

Early one morning, my mom asked me to do some yard work for her.

"Do I have to?" I grumbled.

"Yes, you do," came the answer I had dreaded. Then my mom followed that up with, "If you have a good attitude about it, it will be easier!"

"That's what you think," I mumbled under my breath. I waited and stalled as long as possible, but eventually my mother wouldn't wait any longer. So I shuffled slowly outside. My feet felt very heavy— almost as though there were magnets attached to them and the ground was metal, or like my socks were filled with wet sand. Or maybe my feet were just glued to the ground. I felt miserable.

As I started to work, I could feel my conscience knocking away at the door of my heart. The words, "It will be easier if you have a good attitude," popped back and forth in my head. I knew that my mom was right, but at that moment I would never admit it.

The work was really frustrating. It took me forever to dig through the ground and find the flower bulbs so we could put them away for planting the following year. The muddy dirt seeped through my hands almost as though it was trying to get away from me and my lousy attitude. The whole time, the little voice inside of me kept repeating, *If you change your attitude, it will be easier!*

"Shut up," I yelled, "just shut up!" I couldn't believe it! I was arguing out loud with myself!

After awhile, my better self won the argument. I decided that I had to change my attitude. I have to admit, the minute my attitude changed, the happier I became and the easier my work was. I finished my work humming every dumb song that popped into my head.

As I walked into the house later that day, I turned to Mom who was peeling potatoes and said, "You were right, my work was easier once I changed my attitude." My mom just smiled and said, "I told you. Now go take a bath and help me make dinner."

WHAT??!!

Melea Wendell, 14

What I've Learned So Far . . .

Don't ever be too full for dessert.

Kristi, 10

Never tell your mom her diet's not working.

Mark, 14

Don't pick on your sister when she's holding a baseball bat.

Jordan, 12

Never try to baptize a cat.

Lily, 13

Remember you're never too old to hold your father's hand.

Maggie, 11

Listen to your brain; it has lots of information.

Charity, 7

Stay away from prunes.

Rolland, 9

Forget the cake; go for the icing.

Sheila, 8

Remember the two places you are always welcome—church and Grandma's house.

Johanna, 11

When you believe that something is the end, think of it as a new beginning.

Carly, 13

The person who can't be there right now might be the person you need later.

Frankie, 12

Never leave your sneakers on the lawn because when you go to put them on the next day, you may get a wet surprise.

Amanda, 14

Respect other people's beliefs and opinions.
Think before you act or speak, instead of after.

Emily, 11

No matter how crazy, serious, hard, easy or anything else life may be . . . it's all you have, so have fun!
New friends come, old friends go, but wherever you are, family stays.

Mary, 14

The trouble with quitting is you don't get to see how the story ends.

Alasdair, 15

The best gift you can give is a hug.

Courtney, 15

Never speak badly to your mother before dinner, especially if you know that she has a good dinner waiting for you.

Mihir, 12

Every person in the whole world wants to be loved, even if they say they don't.

Robyn, 12

Somewhere in the world, there is someone else who is less fortunate than you.

Lori, 14

Don't try to brush a dog's teeth when it's mad.
Don't blow bubble-gum bubbles when you are brushing your hair.

Ryann, 9

When you borrow a friend's necklace, don't lose it.
When your baby cousin comes over, lock your bedroom door.
Don't buy things that are just part of a fad.

Aubrie, 10

Never eat Cheetos with braces, no matter how good they are.

Blair, 12

You miss 100 percent of the shots you don't take.

Carly, 12

Growing up is not easy, so don't do it alone.

Amela, 14

Don't interrupt people when they are talking.

Emmy, 9

Never let the fear of striking out keep you from playing the game.

Laura, 13

Some people are always complaining that roses have thorns. I'm just thankful that thorns have roses.

Maddison, 12

Don't be in too much of a rush to grow up. Do you really want to go to work, or take care of yourself when you are sick, or get wrinkles?

Danika, 12

I won't spend my time trying to be popular. I will spend it making good friends.

Tammy, 12

Don't hurt your siblings, and then run away and hide. You'll get in even more trouble.

Morgan, 9, and Raymond, 11 (siblings)

The difference between "ordinary" and "extraordinary" is that little "extra."

Angie, 11

School is cool whether you believe it or not.

Melissa, 11

Never growl at a dog because it could take it as a threat and bite you.

Diego, 13

You don't have to be in a gang to be cool. Just walk away.

Jordana, 10

Never drink grape juice near your older sister before her wedding. She might come down the hall in a purple dress.

Georgia, 11

Lessons for Sale

Experience is a hard teacher because it gives the test first and the lesson afterward.

Vernon Sanders Law

"I'm sooooo bored today!" my sister, Linda, whispered to me during morning recess. "Let's pretend we're sick," she plotted. "Then we can go home and play until Mom and Cheryl get there." Cheryl was our little sister whose kindergarten class was near our mother's office.

"Great!" I squealed, without thinking it through. I adored my big sister and would do anything to be with her.

"Shhhh!" Linda hissed, and then grabbed her belly. "Oooooh, my stomach hurts!"

"Mine, too," I moaned, winking.

Shortly after returning to class, I asked to use the restroom. When I came back, I whimpered with my best tummy-ache look, "I'm feeling sick. I'd better go see the nurse."

"I'm so sorry, honey," Mrs. Brown, my teacher, said.

"Thanks," I whispered, ignoring the voice inside my head that was saying, *Don't do this.*

The nurse asked some questions, had me lie down and gently stroked my head. When she returned thirty minutes later, I told some more lies—BIG ones. I said that I felt worse and that I had just phoned my mother. She was leaving work right away to meet me at home. The nurse checked my file and found a permission slip for me to walk home. Suddenly, the nurse dialed my mother's work number! I gasped and held my breath. After a gazillion rings, she hung up. "No answer. I guess your mom's already heading home. You go straight there, okay?"

"Promise," I replied, flashing a sickly smile, super-relieved that my mother had been away from her desk.

Linda wasn't home when I arrived, but I expected her soon. I couldn't wait to hang out with my big sister! Bored, I opened my lunch sack and ate my bologna sandwich. I imagined my friends in the cafeteria, eating and laughing together. I kept peeking out the window and thinking about what my classmates would be doing later. A film about Mexico, a spelling bee and a math test were planned. *Oh, rats!* We were also going to hear the last chapter of that neat mystery book!

Still no Linda, and nothing to do. I wandered into my mother's bedroom and started going through her stuff. I put on some lipstick, earrings and a long yellow necklace. I took off my school uniform and slipped into one of my mother's bras, her sparkly black dress and some shiny high heels. That got boring fast. I wobbled into the living room and flopped down on the couch in disgust.

Several minutes later, I finally heard a key in the door. Before I could yell at Linda for taking so long, my mouth fell open in shock. Instead of my sister walking into the room, it was my mother! I was speechless and unable to move. Mom strolled over to where I was lying down. "I came home from work to let the plumber in. May I ask what YOU'RE doing here, young lady?"

Swallowing hard, I managed to squeak, "I'm . . . ah . . . sick?"

"Well, you seem well enough to play dress-up," my mother replied calmly.

"I had a tummy-ache, but I'm better now," I answered.

"That's good," my mother responded. "Then you can go back to class, can't you?"

"Yes, ma'am," I sputtered, rising and heading for my room.

"Where do you think you're going?" asked Mom.

"To put my uniform back on."

"No, I think you've missed enough school for one day," she said. "Go get in the car."

Horrified, I squawked, "I CAN'T wear THIS!"

"NOW!!" was the firm reply.

I couldn't believe it. I felt like a zombie and looked

like a clown. That silent two-block drive back to school seemed to last forever. When we parked, Mom got out with me, held my hand like a little kid and marched me into my classroom. My friends burst out laughing, and my mother made me share what I had done. Mrs. Brown looked sad as she asked me to take my seat. I stared at my desk while tears dripped onto my notebook. Now I honestly felt sick, but a different kind of sick.

I heard giggles all afternoon. Even worse, I had to walk home in that outfit, and practically everyone in the whole school saw me. Someone yelled, "Hey, stupid! Halloween is in October!" At the house, I quickly changed clothes and washed off the makeup. When Cheryl and Mom got home, my little sister threw her arms around me happily. All of a sudden I realized that Cheryl probably felt about me the same way that I felt about Linda. I hugged Cheryl tighter than I ever had before.

Linda told me that once she got back into class, she realized what a dumb plan we had made and changed her mind, assuming that I wouldn't go through with it either. She did the right thing, so I couldn't stay mad at her.

At bedtime, Mom kissed us three girls goodnight, leaving our room without saying another word about what happened. When the door closed, I started crying quietly. Sure, I'd be really embarrassed to face my friends tomorrow, but I mostly felt rotten for doing something so stupid—for lying to my sweet teacher and that nice school nurse, for disappointing my mom and making her life harder. When I stopped crying, I could hear both my sisters breathing deeply, already fast asleep . . . and I smiled. I had learned more than one important lesson that day.

Karen Waldman

8

YOU CAN DO IT

You have to have confidence in your own ability, and then be tough enough to follow through.

Rosalyn Carter

The Seed

*I have learned to use the word "impossible"
with great caution.*

Wernher von Braun

I have often been told, "You can't do that." Despite
that, I always reached, dreamed, and wanted to do
things that were said to be impossible or beyond my
ability.

One day, when I was in the fourth grade, our
teacher, Miss Parenzino, took us through the process
of how plants grow. She cut open a dry seed and
showed us how to plant and take care of it. When I
saw the first sprout that came out of the soil a few
weeks later, I was hooked.

On the day of that sprouting, I ran home all excited
and burst into our apartment yelling, "Mama, Mama!
I want to grow an orange tree. I know how." I didn't
want anything small—I wanted to grow a tree. My

mother frowned and said her usual, "You can't do that, Teresa."

I told her I was going to grow an orange tree—no matter what she thought. I was close to tears. She squinted at me to see if I were really serious and said, "Teresa, this is not the climate for growing citrus trees. It's too cold here. Look . . ." She held up an orange she had gotten out of the refrigerator. "This orange is stamped 'Florida.' We live in New York. It's warm all year round in Florida. An orange tree could never grow here in New York because of our cold winters. Maybe this spring you can grow some flowers in a pot."

"No, Mama, I am going to grow an orange tree," I declared. With that, I went to my sunny room and sat on my bed. I ate the orange my mother had shown me and saved one seed. I set it on the windowsill in a jelly jar top to dry. I printed a note and put it next to my treasure, which said, "Private property. Do not touch."

Two weeks later, to my surprise, my mother brought home a large pot and some planting soil. She gave it to me and said, "It's for your seed." I gave my mother a hug that nearly knocked her over.

I split my orange seed and planted it. I watered it and watched. Every day I came home from school and talked to the soil in the pot. I begged and pleaded with the seed to grow. I blessed it and kissed the air around it. My mother just shook her head at me.

One day in early spring, I wandered into my room and looked into the pot. There it was! A little green sprout! My throat felt tight, and I felt like crying for joy.

When my mother came home from work that night, I danced all around her and kissed her hand. Amusement transformed her face, and her exhaustion disappeared. I dragged her to my window. She looked into the pot, and her mouth opened. "I told you, Mama. I told you," I said, as she smiled.

I showered my little sprout with love. It returned my love by growing more and more. Green branches started to stretch their arms. Leaves appeared on the branches. A few months later, the tree grew so big that a decision had to be made. Max, the old barber down the street, was willing to put the tree in his shop window. Max and I planted my little "soul tree" in a larger container, and I continued to care for it.

I grew taller, and so did the orange tree. To my delight, my tree grew little oranges, and its beauty filled the whole window. The tree grew to be so big that Max had to transplant it to his backyard. I felt sad that my tree was now so many blocks away, but I had a feeling that my tree would always remember me. After all, I was the one who loved it so much that it grew where it wasn't supposed to grow.

I no longer live in New York, but my orange tree still lives in Max's backyard. It had started its life as a seed, and that seed taught me many things. I learned that I could do things that I didn't think I could do or that others told me were impossible. My orange tree and the experience of overcoming the odds of growing it will always be in my heart.

Teresa Sendra-Anagnost

Helping Hungry Kids

One October morning, our Sunday school teacher said something that made me sit up and listen.

"Who would like to volunteer to help hungry kids in other countries?" she asked.

My hand shot up. Lately, I had been worrying a lot about kids in Africa. Some of them had to sort through garbage to find food. Many did not go to school. The photographs that bothered me the most were kids so skinny you could see their ribs.

"Anyone else?" The teacher stood with her arms folded across her chest.

No one else raised a hand.

After class, the teacher found me. "Oh, J. J., thanks for offering to help."

"Um . . . I'm not quite sure about what you said I would be doing. Would you go over it again?"

"Well, you'll go door-to-door tonight and ask for money that will be sent to help hungry children in other parts of the world."

"Cool," I replied, feeling better. I really did care about hungry kids. Then I realized she had said *tonight*. Tonight was Halloween! I had planned on going trick-or-treating with my friend, Jackie, and wearing my new witch costume. But before I could explain, she handed me a yellow bag and left the room.

In the bag, I found a paper telling me what to say to people, and a can with a picture of a starving child on it. That's when I started to cry.

By the time I got home, my tears were gone. Mom was standing in the kitchen doorway when she spotted the bag. "What are you doing with that?" she asked.

"I'm going to collect money tonight," I replied, "for starving kids in other countries."

"I thought you were going trick-or-treating with Jackie tonight."

"Starving children are more important," I replied.

"Well, that changes my plans. I'll have to go with you, and you are going to have to figure out what you are going to tell Jackie."

Jackie was my best friend, and I had never let her down. Never.

I called up Jackie, and we figured out that I could still go trick-or-treating with her if I wore the ghost costume she had used a couple of years ago. I'd rush over to her house after my mom and I were done collecting money, and I could just throw the ghost costume over my head. That way I wouldn't have to take a lot of time putting on green makeup so I would look like a witch.

After I hung up the phone, I read the papers from the yellow bag again so I would remember what to say when the first door opened. I imagined the sound of coins clinking into the can. Then I took one more look at the starving boy pictured on the can and reminded myself about why I was doing this.

By the time Mom and I left, the sun was setting. At the first house, my mom waited on the sidewalk, and I went up to the door and rang the bell.

The door opened, and a voice from behind the screen door said, "Yes?"

"My name is J. J., and I am asking my neighbors to donate . . ."

The door slammed in my face.

As Mom and I walked away, I told myself not to take it personally. The person behind that door didn't even know why I was collecting money.

Thinking of the hungry kids, I marched up to the next house. No one was home.

At the third house, a grinning pumpkin let out a scary laugh. I knocked on the door, and a tiny woman with a wrinkled face answered. She listened quietly, and when I was done, she disappeared. I waited, holding my can in front of me, just in case. She came back and put something into the can. It did not make a clink. When I looked at it later, she had put in a ten-dollar bill!

With Mom trailing behind me, I ran as fast as I could

from house to house to collect more donations before it got too dark. By the time the trick-or-treaters started to appear, I had a full can of donations— enough to feed a lot of kids.

We hurried home, and I left the can of money in a safe place. Then I rushed over to Jackie's. I planned to ask her if she wanted my witch costume. I already knew that I wasn't going to have time to put it on next year either.

To me, helping hungry kids brought me more joy than getting dressed up as a scary witch.

J. J. Kay

The Deal

I have always been very close to my grandpa. He would come over every weekend to play with me, and I would call him on the telephone every night just to see what he was doing.

When I was five years old, my grandpa had a heart attack. My mother got to go to the hospital, but I had to stay home. When my grandpa started feeling better, I was able to visit him at the hospital. I was scared to see him, but also very excited, so I ran over and gave him a big hug. I was so glad that he was going to be okay. We talked about what had happened to him and why. Grandpa had smoked cigarettes for a long time, and the doctors knew that that was part of the reason he got sick. That's when I came up with a plan.

"Grandpa, if I stop sucking my thumb, would you please stop smoking?" I asked. I knew that would be very hard for me to do because I really enjoyed sucking my thumb. But my mom would often tell me that if I kept sucking my thumb, over time, it could make my teeth stick out. I knew that it would be best for me to stop.

I also knew that it would not be easy for my grandpa to quit smoking because he had done it for years. I was told that the habit of smoking is very hard to break. But my grandpa agreed, and so we decided to break a habit that would be very hard for each of us.

For a few weeks, I put something over my thumb every night when I went to bed. Slowly I was able to get through the night without anything on it at all. It was very hard for me at first, but it has been about three years now, and I have not sucked my thumb since that night at the hospital. The best part is that my grandpa hasn't smoked anymore either.

I am so lucky to still have my grandpa. I only wish he could have learned about the harmful effects of smoking earlier. Because he smoked for so many years, he has done a lot of harm to his body, and after he got better from his heart attack, he got throat cancer. Now he has trouble even drinking water. It makes me sad to see my grandpa in so much pain.

But I have learned some great lessons from all of this. I learned that people can change if they really try. Hopefully, people will make choices to quit bad habits before it's too late.

Andrea Reese, 8

I Will Succeed

No one knows what he can do until he tries.

Publilius Syrus

It happened the summer between the end of second grade and the beginning of third grade.

Out of the blue, I started twitching my right hand, blowing on my fingers, kicking out my legs while watching TV and, worst of all, walking in little circles and twirling around before I could sit down. This might not sound bad, but I did it every few minutes. My sisters laughed at me and teased me about it. My relatives just thought I was trying to act weird to get attention. My mom got worried.

Luckily, my dad is the kind of doctor who knows a lot about nerves, brains and that kind of stuff. He started watching me closely and reading all of his medical books. He decided that I have a nervous disorder called Tourette's Syndrome. Tourette's is a problem where a person moves in ways that he can't control. Sometimes, people with Tourette's have voice problems called "vocal tics."

After I had the moving problems, I started having vocal tics, too. I grunted and cleared my throat all the time. My mom had to tell my teachers about it, just in case I might disturb the class. I made it through third grade pretty well. It was during fourth grade that it got kind of bad.

I got the flu and a bad cough and couldn't stop clearing my throat all the time. I couldn't help myself. I sounded like I was choking, but I didn't realize that I was even doing anything. My teachers went crazy and asked my mom to please, please take me to a doctor or do *something!* I was constantly being reminded to try to stop making noises or asked to leave the room. I felt very bad, and I was angry at everyone because it wasn't something that I could control. I realized then that I did have a handicap, and it bothered a lot of people. Eventually, I got over the cough, and I did have to take some medicine to help. After about two months, the throat-clearing finally stopped.

I figured out that my "tics" act up worse when I'm tired, sick, stressed out about school or very excited about something. Knowing how to try and avoid those things helps.

My dad said that a lot of kids who have Tourette's have attention problems and usually have a hard time learning and studying. I didn't want that to happen to me, so I tried to concentrate my hardest, and did my homework and projects the best I could. I made really high marks on my fourth-grade testing, and I was recommended to be tested for the Gifted Program. I took that test and scored way high. I was so proud!

That was just a few months ago, so now I will be in the special Gifted/Talented Program at school next year. I am so happy that all my hard work paid off! I am also in the top of my violin class, and I play piano, too.

I know I have a handicap, but now it doesn't seem so bad. My dad says it might go away as I grow older— but it could also get worse. I guess we won't know until time goes by. After learning more about how to deal with my problem, I'm finding that I can control it a little better, and I am determined to succeed!

I just want other kids to know that even if you have a handicap, you can really try hard and make yourself stronger in other ways. You can pretty much do whatever you set your mind to. GO FOR IT! That's what I'm doing.

Elizabeth Jules, 10

[EDITORS' NOTE: *For more information about Tourette's Syndrome, go to* www.tsa-usa.org.]

Swish

Perseverance is failing nineteen times and succeeding the twentieth.

Julie Andrews

I was seven years old when I first started playing basketball. Most of the time you could find me sitting on the bench—I only played, like, one minute in each of the games. One day at practice, the best player on the team sprained his ankle. Our coach told me to fill the position of forward. I asked him, "Are you sure?" His answer was that he had a lot of confidence in me. That one comment gave me the courage to do what I had to do—I guarded my man and got a lot of rebounds. We were almost done with practice when my friend, Max, passed me the ball. That's when I realized I had never made a basket before.

I threw the ball, hoping it would go in—but it didn't. That afternoon, Coach showed me how to bend my wrist back and let the ball roll off my fingers. He told me that I needed to practice because the championship game was coming up.

For the next two weeks I practiced, rain or snow. My dad was very proud of me for practicing that hard. But . . . I still couldn't make even one basket.

The day of the championship game arrived, and Coach put me in as the starting forward. Throughout the game, our team would score—and then the other team would score and catch up with us. By the fourth quarter, we were tied—sixteen to sixteen. With fifteen seconds left to go on the clock, our team had the ball.

All of a sudden, Coach called for a time-out. He told our team to let me go for the last shot. I said, "What if I miss? I'll let the team down!"

He replied, "It doesn't matter, as long as I know you are willing to give 100 percent. The last few days you have shown your talent. I should have put you in the games way before this. Just remember what I taught you and imagine that it will go into the basket. Now, go for it!"

We went back onto the court. The clock was down to ten seconds when the ball was passed to me. I dribbled and got up as far as the free-throw line. I had an open shot, so I pulled back and just let the ball roll off my fingers like I had done in my practices. As the ball left my fingers, I said, "Swish!" The ball went flying, then—*swish*—the ball went in.

We had won the game, 18–16!

Everyone was proud of me, especially Coach and

my parents. My job was done, and I felt like a million dollars.

And that is how I became the great basketball player that I am today.

SWISH!

Ruben Ray Garcia Jr., 13

Katie

Energy and persistence conquer all things.

Benjamin Franklin

I have a big family: a brother, Scott, two sisters, Katie and Shannon, and our mom and dad. Everybody in the family has taken, or is currently taking, piano lessons. My brother has taken lessons for eight years, my sister Shannon has taken them for ten years, Mom for two years, Dad for nine, and I have taken lessons for four years. Even my grandmother took lessons. My sister Katie has taken lessons for eleven years.

Katie is unique. Because she can't hear as well as the rest of us, she wears a hearing aid. She can't hear the snap of a finger or the pretty songs of the birds in the morning. She has trouble hearing the highest notes in the pieces she plays on the piano. Sometimes we have to repeat what we're saying or a joke that everybody's laughing at so that she can join in the laughter.

There is something else that makes it even harder for Katie. You see, Katie was born with only four fingers. Because of this, Katie has to practice twice as much as the rest of us. I can't imagine what it must be like for her—not only how hard it would be to play the piano with only four fingers, but also how difficult it would be if I was unable to hear even everyday sounds.

Despite everything she has had to endure, Katie has never given up and never stopped learning to play the piano. I'm thankful to have such a great sister and that she sets a good example for the rest of us.

Christopher McConaughy, 10

Reaching Goals

Goals are dreams that you set for yourself.
It may be an award that sits on a shelf,
To become famous with tons of fans,
Or even to be brave enough to make a stand.
If you fail, don't give up, just try again.
You'll realize your dream in the end.
Believe in yourself, and you will succeed,
Because self-confidence is all that you need.
Don't listen to what other people say.
You won't get anywhere doing it that way.
Know that you can do it, don't have a doubt.
Smile at your fears, that's what it's about.
The sky is the limit, there are no rules.
Brainpower, confidence, these are the tools.
So set some goals and get out there today,
Go out into the world and be on your way.

Emma West, 12

Proving Them Wrong

By perseverance the snail reached the ark.

Charles Haddon Spurgeon

Only three more miles, I thought, . . . *only three.*

There were a lot of people running in front of me, and not too many people running in back of me. I wasn't the slowest runner, but then again a ten-year-old kid usually isn't the fastest runner competing against a bunch of twenty-year-olds—with even some older, professional runners in the race. Also, I am not a very fast runner because one of my legs is shorter than the other.

When I was born, I had a tumor in my lower spine that pressed on my nerves and caused me to be paralyzed from the waist down. The doctors told my parents that they didn't think that I would be able to walk—let alone run. I had to have a lot of surgeries over the next several years. During that time, I decided that I would prove the doctors were wrong. I *did* walk. And not only did I walk, I learned how to run! I just don't have the ability to run as fast as other kids.

So let's just say that when it came to running a race, I wasn't usually one of the first ten kids to finish—or even one of the first twenty. But because of my determination, I also wasn't the last.

So here I was, running a 5K for Girls On the Run, International, a program that encourages positive, healthy ways of living while training girls to run. A lot of my girlfriends were running in this race, so I decided to run too. For several weeks, we had trained hard to get where we were on the day of the race.

When the buzzer sounded to signal the beginning, my friends Shayna and Melissa started running beside me. But then Melissa, wanting to run alone, ran up farther. Shayna stayed with me. We ran as fast as we could up the hill. Then Shayna went a little farther ahead of me, but she stayed close enough so that I could still see her.

When we had two more miles to go, we stopped at the high school. I got a drink of water, which refreshed my body and gave me more energy. I reminded myself, *Only two more miles.* Again I ran, the wind carrying me.

Then the clouds got really dark, and it started to rain. *No,* I thought, *not now! I only have one more mile.* As I got closer to the finish line, it began to really pour. The rain made it hard for me to see, but I stayed focused on my goal. I believed that I could finish the race—rain or no rain!

As I started to pass where my mom and family were standing and watching, my mom came over to me, pulled me out of the street and said, "Come on, let's go." I think she thought that the race had already ended. But I pulled away from her and pointed to the sign ahead that marked the finish line. Then I sprinted toward it with all my might!

I was only ten seconds . . . nine seconds . . . five seconds away! I was one second away . . . then I was . . . *there!*

I collapsed just a few feet beyond the finish line, completely drenched from the rain. *See,* I thought, *I could do it. I really could! I only wish that those doctors could have seen me run!* After I caught my breath, I got up and ran back to my mom.

Of course, taking forty-five minutes to run three miles isn't really the best time, but hey—I did it! Now I'm thirteen, and I know that if I run again, I can do even better than that. You never know, one day I could run the ten-mile race in New York.

And I could win.

Sara Alpert, 13

Afterword

It is our hope that these stories have brought you hope, joy, courage and inspiration, and that they will live on through you. You are now the storyteller. May they continue to touch you and empower you.

Big Brothers Big Sisters

Big Brothers Big Sisters Association is a nonprofit organization dedicated to mentoring at-risk youth and helping them overcome the many challenges they face. Founded in 1904, Big Brothers Big Sisters is the oldest and largest youth mentoring organization in the United States.

Research shows that youth who are mentored through the BBBS program are less likely to begin using illegal drugs, consume alcohol, skip school, or engage in acts of violence. They have greater self-esteem, confidence in their schoolwork performance, and are able to get along better with their friends and families.

The organization serves more than 225,000 youth ages five through eighteen, in 5,000 communities across the country, through a network of 470 agencies. For more information about Big Brothers Big Sisters, or to find an agency near you, please visit *www.bbbsa.org,* or contact:

Big Brothers Big Sisters National Office
230 North 13th Street
Philadelphia, PA 19107
(215) 567-7000
www.bbbsa.org

Who Is Jack Canfield?

Jack Canfield is one of America's leading experts in the development of human potential and personal effectiveness. He is both a dynamic, entertaining speaker and a highly sought-after trainer. Jack has a wonderful ability to inform and inspire audiences toward increased levels of self-esteem and peak performance.

He is the author and narrator of several bestselling audio- and videocassette programs, including *Self-Esteem and Peak Performance, How to Build High Self-Esteem, Self-Esteem in the Classroom* and *Chicken Soup for the Soul—Live.* He is regularly seen on television shows such as *Good Morning America, 20/20* and *NBC Nightly News.* Jack has co-authored numerous books, including the *Chicken Soup for the Soul* series, *Dare to Win* and *The Aladdin Factor* (all with Mark Victor Hansen), *100 Ways to Build Self-Concept in the Classroom* (with Harold C. Wells), *Heart at Work* (with Jacqueline Miller) and *The Power of Focus* (with Les Hewitt and Mark Victor Hansen).

Jack is a regularly featured speaker for professional associations, school districts, government agencies, churches, hospitals, sales organizations and corporations. His clients have included the American Dental Association, the American Management Association, AT&T, Campbell's Soup, Clairol, Domino's Pizza, GE, ITT, Hartford Insurance, Johnson & Johnson, the Million Dollar Roundtable, NCR, New England Telephone, Re/Max, Scott Paper, TRW and Virgin Records. Jack has taught on the faculty of Income Builders International, a school for entrepreneurs.

Jack conducts an annual seven-day Training of Trainers program in the areas of self-esteem and peak performance. It attracts entrepreneurs, educators, counselors, parenting trainers, corporate trainers, professional speakers, ministers and others interested in developing their speaking and seminar-leading skills.

For further information about Jack's books, tapes and training programs, or to schedule him for a presentation, please contact:

Self-Esteem Seminars
P.O. Box 30880
Santa Barbara, CA 93130
phone: 805-563-2935 • fax: 805-563-2945
Website: *www.jackcanfield.com*

Who Is Mark Victor Hansen?

In the area of human potential, no one is more respected than Mark Victor Hansen. For more than thirty years, Mark has focused solely on helping people from all walks of life reshape their personal vision of what's possible. His powerful messages of possibility, opportunity and action have created powerful change in thousands of organizations and millions of individuals worldwide.

He is a sought-after keynote speaker, bestselling author and marketing maven. Mark's credentials include a lifetime of entrepreneurial success and an extensive academic background. He is a prolific writer with many bestselling books, such as *The One Minute Millionaire, The Power of Focus, The Aladdin Factor* and *Dare to Win,* in addition to the *Chicken Soup for the Soul* series. Mark has made a profound influence through his library of audios, videos and articles in the areas of big thinking, sales achievement, wealth building, publishing success, and personal and professional development.

Mark is the founder of the MEGA Seminar Series. MEGA Book Marketing University and Building Your MEGA Speaking Empire are annual conferences where Mark coaches and teaches new and aspiring authors, speakers and experts on building lucrative publishing and speaking careers. Other MEGA events include MEGA Marketing Magic and My MEGA Life.

He has appeared on television (*Oprah, CNN* and *The Today Show*), in print (*Time, U.S. News & World Report, USA Today, New York Times* and *Entrepreneur*) and on countless radio interviews, assuring our planet's people that "You can easily create the life you deserve."

As a philanthropist and humanitarian, Mark works tirelessly for organizations such as Habitat for Humanity, American Red Cross, March of Dimes, Childhelp and many others. He is the recipient of numerous awards that honor his entrepreneurial spirit, philanthropic heart and business acumen. He is a lifetime member of the Horatio Alger Association of Distinguished Americans, an organization that honored Mark with the prestigious Horatio Alger Award for his extraordinary life achievements.

Mark Victor Hansen is an enthusiastic crusader of what's possible and is driven to make the world a better place.

Mark Victor Hansen & Associates, Inc.
P.O. Box 7665
Newport Beach, CA 92658
phone: 949-764-2640
fax: 949-722-6912
Website: *www.markvictorhansen.com*

Who Is Patty Hansen?

Patty Hansen, with her partner Irene, authored *Chicken Soup for the Kid's Soul, Chicken Soup for the Preteen Soul I* and *II, Chicken Soup Christmas Treasury for Kids* and *Chicken Soup for the Girl's Soul*—all books that kids ages nine through thirteen love to read and use as guides for everyday life. Patty is also a contributor to some of the most loved stories in the *Chicken Soup for the Soul* series; co-author of *Condensed Chicken Soup for the Soul* (Health Communications, Inc.) and *Out of the Blue: Delight Comes into Our Lives* (HarperCollins).

Because of her love for preteens, Patty created *www.Preteenplanet.com*, a Website to give preteens a fun and safe cyberspace experience where they can also become empowered to make their world a better place. Check it out!

Prior to her career as an author, Patty worked for United Airlines as a flight attendant for thirteen years. During that time, she received two commendations for bravery. She received the first one when (as the only flight attendant on board) she prepared forty-four passengers for a successful planned emergency landing. The second was for singlehandedly extinguishing a fire on board a mid-Pacific flight, thus averting an emergency situation and saving hundreds of lives.

Patty is the president of legal and licensing for Chicken Soup for the Soul Enterprises, Inc., helping to create an entire line of *Chicken Soup for the Soul* products and licenses.

Patty shares her home life with her two daughters, Elisabeth and Melanie; grandson, Seth; her mother, Shirley; housekeeper and friend, Eva; two rabbits, four horses, three dogs, six cats, four birds, thirty-two fish, eight pigeons, thirty-six chickens (yes, they all have names), a haven for hummingbirds and a butterfly farm.

If you would like to contact Patty:
Patty Hansen
P.O. Box 10879
Costa Mesa, CA 92627
E-mail: *patty@preteenplanet.com*
Website: *www.preteenplanet.com*

Who Is Irene Dunlap?

Irene Dunlap, co-author of *Chicken Soup for the Kid's Soul, Chicken Soup for the Preteen Soul, Chicken Soup for the Soul Christmas Treasury for Kids, Chicken Soup for the Preteen Soul 2* and *Chicken Soup for the Girl's Soul* began her writing career in elementary school when she discovered her love for creating poetry, a passion she believes to have inherited from her paternal grandmother. She went on to express her love for words through writing fictional short stories, lyrics, as a participant in speech competitions and eventually as a vocalist.

During her college years, Irene traveled around the world as a student of the Semester at Sea program aboard a ship that served as a classroom, as well as home base, for over 500 college students. After earning a Bachelor of Arts degree in Communications, she became the Media Director of Irvine Meadows Amphitheatre in Irvine, California, and eventually co-owned an advertising and public-relations agency that specialized in entertainment and health-care clients.

Irene released her first book in a series titled *TRUE—Real Stories About God Showing Up in the Lives of Teens* in February 2004, in order to encourage teens and young adults in their faith. While creating difference-making books, which she sees as a blessing, Irene continues to support her two teens with their interests while she carries on a singing career, performing various styles ranging from jazz to contemporary music at church and special events.

Irene lives in Newport Beach, California, with her husband, Kent, daughter, Marleigh, son, Weston, and Australian Shepherd, Gracie. In her spare time, Irene enjoys horseback riding, gardening, cooking and painting. If you are wondering how she does it all, she will refer you to her favorite Bible passage for her answer—Ephesians 3:20.

If you would like to contact Irene, write to her at:

Irene Dunlap
P.O. Box 10879
Costa Mesa, CA 92627
E-mail: *irene@lifewriters.com*
Website: *www.LifeWriters.com*

Who Are the Chicken Soup for the Soul® Souper Kids

Chicken Soup for the Soul®

Presents

Souper Kids™

Chicken Soup for the Soul Souper Kids™

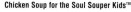

**They're schoolmates, playmates, come-what-may-mates.
Buds for life, they're "Souper" soul mates.
Friends like family, tight like glue.
And "Souper" good is what they're out to do.
Here they come—six kids, one dog, one chicken . . .
and a whole lot of love'n fun.**

Crystal

When Crystal loves something, she REALLY loves it! She's crazy about new hair-dos, the color pink and taking pictures with her ever-present cell phone. Crystal's heart is as big as can be—nobody jumps to help her friends faster than Crystal.

The Twins

Ricardo and Roberto. They look alike, dress alike, walk alike, and sometimes even talk alike—but they're as different as night and day. Ricardo's our "break-up-the-class" clown and Roberto's our quiet poet and songwriter. Who's their best audience? Each other, of course!

Samara

Samara's all imagination, creativity, spirit and wild ideas. Who knows what she'll think of next! "Let's decorate our backpacks. . . . Let's make friendship bracelets. . . . Let's all write a book together." There's never a dull moment when Samara's around.

O'Brien

O'Brien . . . Oh boy! She's a tomboy rebel with a heart, our tough and tender activist. Today it's save the whales, tomorrow it's save the planet. Step back and watch O'Brien make it happen. She's out to change the world, and, knowing her, she just might do it!

Chester

Our favorite brainiac . . . with an off-beat, oddball sense of humor. He'll rebuild your computer, rewire your cell phone and help you with your homework. Who's his best bud? His pet chicken, Poulet, of course.

Poulet

Chester's other half. A peckin', scratchin', dancin', struttin' chicken. But if you think he's just an ordinary bird-brain, think again. Poulet's practically psychic.

Farley

Farley is everybody's dog. He's all heart (and appetite). He's the original walk-into-the-wall goof-ball. But you can't help loving him. Scratch his tummy and you've got a friend for life.

Watch for the Souper Kids in upcoming *Chicken Soup for the Soul* books and products. As an added bonus we have included the Chicken Soup for the Soul Souper Kids Color Cartoon Collection.

The Chicken Soup
for the Soul® Souper Kids
Cartoon Collection

Get a Free Poster!

Here's your chance to get a free mini-poster of the Souper Kids for your room! Go to *www.chickensoup.com/poster* to order.

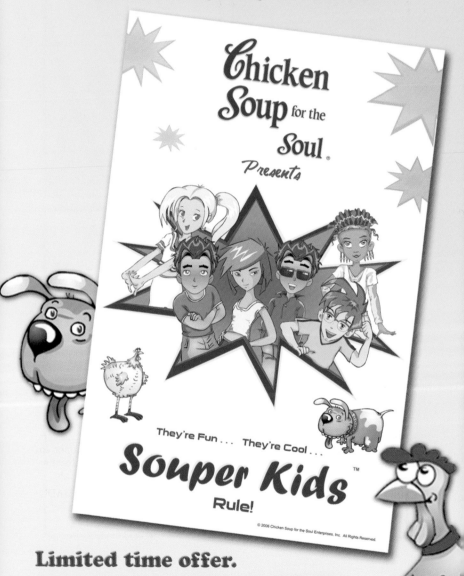

Limited time offer.

Poster size is 11"x17". $3.95 shipping and handling will be charged.* Must be 18 years or older to order. If you're under 18 and want to order, let Mom, Dad or another adult help you!

Contributors

The stories in the book were submitted by kids and adults who have read our previous *Chicken Soup for the Soul* books and who responded to our request for stories. We have included information about these authors and contributors below.

Sara Alpert is in the eighth grade, and enjoys writing and acting. She plans on being a lawyer and an author.

Alese Bagdol is a senior in high school and the Assistant Editor-in-Chief of her school newspaper. She is involved in dance, and enjoys skiing, cooking and traveling. She aspires to work as a magazine editor in the future.

Chrissy Booth is a senior in high school and will graduate in May 2006. She has been writing since she was quite young and was first published in third grade. Her plans for college include the study of medicine and theology.

Alison Braneim is thirteen years old, and enjoys singing, reading, writing and discovering things about herself. She hopes that her story will inspire kids to be themselves and to make friends who appreciate them for who they are.

Rosemary K. Breckler has had two stories published in *Highlights for Children* and later published *Where Are the Twins?*, a HiLo mystery novel. She wrote *Hoang Breaks the Lucky Teapot* and *Sweet Dried Apples*, two books about children in Vietnam during the war. For eight years she was a volunteer "grandma" for a public library.

Alyse Cleaver is a second-year graduate student at the University of Massachusetts–Dartmouth. She received her Bachelor of Science degree in Physiology from Michigan State University and is now pursuing a Master of Arts degree in Professional Writing from UMass–Dartmouth. In her spare time she enjoys listening to music and concerts, and hopes to write for a music-related magazine.

Alanah Coggins is an eighth-grade student who is involved in softball and volleyball. She especially loves music and going to concerts. She hopes to attend Central Michigan University and become a special-education teacher because of her experience with J. W.

Caitlin Conley attends high school where she is active in band and SADD (Students Against Destructive Decisions). Her hobbies include reading, writing and listening to music.

Jessica Crown is a student in public high school in Oregon. She is a varsity cheerleader and plays softball during the spring. Jessica enjoys music, art and the outdoors. She loves animals and would like to someday work with animals as a veterinarian.

Mary Lou De Caprio graduated with a Bachelor of Science in Chemistry with honors from Fairleigh Dickinson University in 1984. She is a substitute elementary schoolteacher and a freelance writer. She enjoys playing piano, volunteering, and doing cool stuff with her husband and four children.

Brandon Deitrick is currently studying Musical Theater at Anne Arundel Community College with hopes to be a Broadway actor. He enjoys dancing and singing in his spare time. He also loves teaching kids the fundamentals of theater through workshops.

Moira Rose Donohue is a reformed lawyer who secretly loves grammar and punctuation. Her first children's book, *Alfie the Apostrophe,* will be published in spring 2006. Moira lives in northern Virginia, and loves her husband, two children and tap dancing. Visit her Website at www.moirarosedonohue.net.

Katy S. Duffield is the author of the picture book, *Farmer McPeepers and His Missing Milk Cows.* Katy's work has also appeared in many magazines, including *Highlights for Children, Family Fun, Guideposts for Kids, Clubhouse, Boys' Quest* and many others. Please visit her Website at *www.katyduffield.com.*

Lauren Durant is a seventh-grade student from a rural city in western Canada who enjoys music and swimming. Lauren, who published her first story at the young age of seven, believes there are many great stories waiting for a gifted storyteller to share.

Tatiana Eugenia is a seventh-grader who lives in Ottawa, Canada, who enjoys writing stories and sharing her experiences. She also enjoys swimming, skiing and skating.

Kate E. Frezon is a junior at Cornell Universtity who is studying Information Sciences and hopes to design Web pages. She enjoys reading and theater, and has been the stage manager of several Cornell productions. Katie has also ushered for shows on Broadway!

Margaret S. (Peggy) Frezon is a freelance writer living in upstate New York. Her work has appeared in *Teaching Tolerance, Positive Thinking and Angels on Earth,* and she's a frequent contributor to *Guideposts* and *Sweet 16.* She enjoys spending time with her family and two dogs, Kelly and Hudson. E-mail her at *ecritMeg@nycap.rr.com.*

Ruben Garcia, Jr. has grown up since writing his story and is now pursuing a career as an electrician. He is looking toward his future as he attends college for a Masters degree. Ruben has since given up sports, but like in his story, the determination and passion are still there.

Donna Getzinger is an award-winning author of thirteen published books for children, and numerous magazine and anthology publications, which includes a story in *Chicken Soup for the Mother's Soul.* For more information about her work, she can be reached at *ringletred@aol.com.*

Eileen M. Hehl was a loving grandmother who found joy in stories told by her grandchildren. She loved this story starring her granddaughter Grace, which she submitted to *Chicken Soup for the Kid's Soul* a few months before she passed away.

Teresa Hosier is a native to Colorado and mother of two, Bailey and Kaleb. She enjoys writing, family time and outdoors. She thanks her mother, Dora, for her lessons in life. Now living in Montana, please write her at 5376 Buttercup

Lane, Florence, MT 59825. She loves mail and will write back personally.

Diana L. James is an author, speaker and compiler of the *Bounce Back* series of books. She lives in Idaho near her four sons and seven grandchildren. Chrissy is one of those grandchildren. Diana's goal in all of her writing and speaking is to give the reader, or audience, words of encouragement, hope and perhaps a good laugh.

Jaime Johnson, M.S., works as a research assistant in the medical field. She also works as a freelance medical editor. Jaime enjoys yoga, dance, reading and writing. She has two short stories published to date and an inspirational book for young women in progress. Please e-mail her at *numinadea@yahoo.com*.

Elizabeth Jules graduated from high school in June 2005 with a B+ grade average. In high school, she enjoyed volunteering and aiding with special-education kids. She enjoys traveling, camping and shopping! After traveling abroad, she plans to attend college and study education.

J. J. Kay lives in south Florida where she writes stories and books for middle-grade readers. She also writes about sailing and traveling with her Lab named Schooner. She and Schooner participate in reading programs and visit the elderly. Write to her at *janice@aposner.net*.

Amanda Kelly attends high school in Ontario, Canada. She enjoys playing the piano, basketball and reading. Her favorite author is Jane Austen. Amanda recently returned from a mission trip to Zambia, Africa, where she worked with orphans and widows in the community.

Heather Klassen writes fiction for children and teenagers from her home in Edmonds, Washington. She enjoys reading, swimming and working with children. You can e-mail her at *tressen60@cs.com*.

Gayle C. Krause has taught Early Childhood Education for thirty years and plans to pursue a full-time career as a writer. A member of the Society of Children's Book Writers and Illustrators, she has attended numerous writing conferences and seminars, and looks forward to using her teaching expertise in creating well-developed, imaginative stories for children.

Virginia Kroll has had forty-seven children's books published since 1992 and over 1,700 items in magazines. She is married and lives in Hamberg, New York, with her family, which includes three daughters, three sons, a granddaughter and thirty-six pets.

Beth Savitz Laliberte received her Bachelor of Science in Physical Therapy from Temple University College of Allied Health Professions and is now practicing at the Jersey shore. She is a former coach and official of Wheelchair Sports competitions. Her husband, Todd, and children, Ryan and Jenny, are her forever inspiration. E-mail her at *gonesailing@optonline.net*.

Karen L. Landrum teaches yoga in the Greater Cincinnati/N. Kentucky area. She began writing as a teen, and continues to enjoy the process of writing and sharing reflections on her Website, *www.writeheart.com*. She has published a story, *A Leap of Faith*, in the book, *You Look Too Young to Be a Mom*, edited by Deborah Davis. She also writes articles for a local Catholic newspaper, *The Messenger*.

Laura Ann Lee is a student in high school who enjoys reading, writing and taking pictures. She wants to become a director of motion pictures and plans to continue to write.

Molly Lemmons is a professional storyteller and the author of *Kind of Heart*, published in 2000, and *The Passing of Paradise*, an inspirational romance released in April 2005. Since retiring from twenty-two years with the Mustang, Oklahoma, public schools, Molly now spends her time traveling and telling stories from her *Kind of Heart* book.

Karen V. Lombard is an economics professor at Chapman University in Orange, California, where she aims to use the lessons she learned from Sister Joanne back in the first grade. She loves writing, especially for children, and spending time with her husband, Alex, and four-year old son, Geordie.

Rachel A. Maddix, author of "A Life Saved," is an ordinary Michigan college student attempting to live an extraordinary life. Rachel enjoys photography, Website design and living the good life. She hopes to one day open a coffee shop or take up salsa and retreat to Bora Bora. Send e-mail to *lanternhorn@gmail.com.*

Nancy Mikaelian Madey is a freelance writer/editor for several national publications, and published author of her own true story, *Facing Fear: A Young Woman's Personal Account of Surviving Breast Cancer.* Her book is available by order only from traditional and online bookstores (ISBN 0-595-15117-5) or at *www.survivingbreastcancer.com.* Nancy is a native of Racine, Wisconsin, and holds a B.A. in Mass Communications from the University of Wisconsin–Milwaukee. She lives in Huntington Beach, California, with her husband and two children.

Christopher McConaughy is a fifteen-year-old who lives in Ohio and attends a Christian school. He enjoys football and basketball, and loves Christian rock, including bands like Pillar and others.

Theresa (Terri) Meehan shares memories of her childhood in "Herbie, Come Home." She resides in England with her husband and likes writing inspiring stories. Many have been published, including poetry for an upcoming *Chicken Soup for the Soul* book.

Christine Middleton received her Bachelor of Arts in Child and Youth Care from the University of Victoria in 1999. This wife and mother is presently working with youth at a middle school. Christine is an aspiring writer of children's stories and short novels for youth. Please e-mail her at *mcmiddleton@shaw.ca.*

Cara Mulhall, age fifteen, is a freshman in high school from Kentucky who enjoys playing softball and going to concerts. Cara wants to be a teacher or a professional writer when she gets older.

JoAnn Palombo lives in New York with her family and one very old dog for whom yawning is active exercise. She found telling this story extremely therapeutic and probably can't be stopped from committing more life experiences to paper. You can reach *JoAnn at jpp109@optonline.net.*

Kathleen Whitman Plucker is a native of Tennessee and received her Bachelor of Arts and Master of Education from the University of Virginia. She now lives in the Midwest. Formerly a Web application developer, Kathleen is a stay-at-home mother and part-time writer. Please e-mail her at *kplucker@earthlink.net.*

Grace Presnick is a seventh-grade student elected to Student Council, appointed as Peer Mediator, state champ soccer goalie, basketball and softball player, and active in her church Youth Ministry. She loves beach vacations with her cousins and skiing with friends. Grace loves to write, just like Grandma Eileen did.

Yvonne Prinz is the author of *Still There, Clare,* the first in a series of books about a twelve-year-old girl and her precocious imaginary friend, Elsa. The second book in the Series, *Not Fair, Clare,* is due out in the fall of 2006. A TV series based on the books is also in the works. Yvonne lives in northern California.

Emily J. Puffpaff, age fourteen, loves to read and write, hang out with her friends and play tennis. She also loves to listen to music and go shopping!

Andrea Reese, a sophomore in high school, enjoys playing soccer for the school and being part of the marching band. She loves hiking up the beautiful Colorado mountains. At the age of eight, she wrote this story and today dedicates it to her grandfather who recently passed away of cancer.

Carla Reimche received her Bachelor of Arts in English from Andrews University in Berrien Springs, Michigan, in 1995, and a Master of Science in Marketing from Johns Hopkins University in Maryland in 2001. Carla specializes in healthcare communications and is happily married with one son. She credits her mother and her favorite English teacher for instilling in her a love for reading and writing.

Emily Rider-Longmaid is a sophomore at Milton Academy. Emily plays soccer and basketball, and is a member of her school's Community Service Board. She enjoys reading, photography and history, and loves spending time with her family and friends.

Michelle Rossi received her Bachelor of Science, with honors, in education from Oakland University in 2004. Michelle is an author of children's and young teen novels. She loves writing, singing, and spending time with family and friends. Please e-mail her at *marross98@wowway.com.*

Ashley Russell is a sophomore in high school who recently finished her freshman year with a 3.83 GPA and is going into English honors. Ashley plans to attend college and major in Psychology. Once her career as a counselor launches, she plans on writing a book about her experiences and theories.

Harriet May Savitz is the author of twenty-two books, including, *Run Don't Walk,* which was made into an ABC Afterschool Special produced by Henry Winkler. She is also co-author (with Ferida Wolff) of a children's picture book called *Is a Worry Worrying You?* (Tanglewood Press). For more information about her children's books, visit her Website at *www.harrietmaysavitz.com.*

Nance Schneider has been teaching for the Appleton Catholic Educational System (ACES) for many years, ranging from grades 3–8. She is currently teaching at St. Joseph Middle School, a campus in the ACES System. Nance enjoys reading, crosswords, cottage life and inspiring children through writing. Please e-mail her at *mickeym275@aol.com.*

Teresa Sendra-Anagnost holds an R.N. degree, and a B.S. and 3/4 B.A. in creative writing from Cal State U. at Northridge. She has been an Advanced Practice Nurse (RNP) for thirty years. Teresa has published poems, articles for professional journals and an entertainment magazine, and enjoys painting, writing stories and reading. E-mail her at *sendag@aol.com.*

Tanya C. Sousa is a guidance counselor and author living in the green mountains of Vermont. She shares a home with three Border Collies, two cats and her husband, John Racine. Tanya writes for publications such as *The Green Mountain Tradinig Post, Dog and Kennel, The Canine Chronical* and *FETCH The Paper,* among others.

April Stier graduated from Bethel College (Indiana) with degrees in English, Biblical Studies, and Professional Writing. Aside from writing and editing, April enjoys reading, hiking, camping, canoeing and watching VeggieTales. You can e-mail her at april_lynn@mac.com.

Kelsey Temple is a sixth-grader who is a straight-A student and is part of the AIG (Academically Intellectually Gifted) program. She enjoys a type of dance called clogging, and collecting keychains and pencils. She has been riding horses since she was three years old, and has won several trophies and ribbons. Kelsey appreciates her family, friends and grandparents who encourage her in everything she does.

Victoria Thornsbury is a first-year student at the Hartt School of Music in Connecticut where she is studying Music Education. She hopes to one day teach her very own children's choir. She enjoys singing, playing the oboe, teaching and writing. You may reach her at *thornsbur@hartford.edu.*

Michael Van Gorder is a sixteen-year-old honors high-school student living in California. He is still fond of dogs, especially his favorite, the Labrador Retriever.

Jean Verwey lives in Cambridge, Ontario. She has published numerous verses for a greeting-card company and enjoys working on her daughter's life book, her writing group and being involved in her church. She and her husband, Mike, have three older children and recently adopted their two-year-old daughter from China.

Zu Vincent holds an MFA in Creative Writing from Vermont College, and writes for both adults and children. Her novel, *The Lucky Place,* will be published by Front Street Press in 2007. She discovered this story while researching and writing a book about animals who have saved their owners' lives.

Karen Waldman, Ph.D., a licensed psychologist, is a frequent contributor to the Chicken Soup series. She enjoys writing poems and stories, dancing, acting, nature, music, traveling with her husband, Ken, spending time with family and friends, and playing with their wonderful children and grandchildren, Natalie, Greta and Lana. E-mail her at *Krobens@aol.com.*

Melea Wendell is currently a student at Oregon State University. She is pursuing a degree in Human Development and Family Sciences and hopes to someday work with children. In the winter of 2006, Melea plans to travel to China and live as a student for an extended period of time. Melea enjoys traveling, writing, snowboarding and a plethora of other activities.

Emma West is a tenth-grade student who enjoys biking, kayaking and golfing, as well as reading, writing, and spending time with her friends and family. Emma will be attending boarding school in the fall and plans to go to a university or college. Emma aspires to be a professional writer, teacher, historian and/or a psychiatrist.